# CLIMATOPOLIS

June 2013,

Dear Sarah,

Have a great summer.

I hope This Book
interests you!

Best,

Matt K~

# CLIMATOPOLIS

*How* OUR CITIES WILL
THRIVE *in*
*the* HOTTER FUTURE

## MATTHEW E. KAHN

BASIC
BOOKS

A Member of the Perseus Books Group
*New York*

Published by Basic Books,
A Member of the Perseus Books Group

Books published by Basic Books are available at special discounts for
bulk purchases in the United States by corporations, institutions, and
other organizations. For more information, please contact the Special
Markets Department at the Perseus Books Group, 2300 Chestnut Street,
Suite 200, Philadelphia, PA 19103, or call (800) 810-4145, ext. 5000, or
e-mail special.markets@perseusbooks.com.

Designed by Pauline Brown
Typeset in 12 point Apollo MT

Library of Congress Cataloging-in-Publication Data
Kahn, Matthew E., 1966–
    Climatopolis : how our cities will thrive in the hotter future /
Matthew E. Kahn.
        p.  cm.
Includes bibliographical references and index.
    ISBN 978-0-465-01926-7 (alk. paper)
    1. Urban ecology (Sociology) 2. City planning—Environmental
aspects. 3. Climate changes. I. Title.
HT241.K338  2010
307.76—dc22

                                                      2010011080

10 9 8 7 6 5 4 3 2

# CONTENTS

**1** TOO MUCH GAS 1

**2** WHAT WE'VE DONE WHEN OUR 15
CITIES HAVE BLOWN UP

**3** KING OF THE HILL 47

**4** PLAYING ONE-ON-ONE 77
WITH KOBE BRYANT

**5** WILL MANHATTAN FLOOD? 111

**6** WILL CHINA'S CITIES GO GREEN? 139

**7** BONO'S ANXIETY 159

**8** SEIZE THE DAY: OPPORTUNITIES 189
FROM OUR HOTTER FUTURE

**9** THE FUTURE OF CITIES 225

ACKNOWLEDGMENTS 245
NOTES 247
SUGGESTED FURTHER READINGS 261
INDEX 263

# CLIMATOPOLIS

# 1

# TOO MUCH GAS

**S**hanghai's growth over the last thirty years has been staggering. Measured in cars, concrete, new buildings, new homes, and air travel, this city has been transformed from an industrial hotbed of revolutionary leftism into one of the world's superstar cities. The neon-lit buildings along its Bund waterfront feature five-star hotels and high-end restaurants such as Jean George—enough in quality and quantity to compete with any other world-class city, from New York to Paris.

The rise of this mega-city foreshadows China's trajectory in the twenty-first century—and that of the rest of the world.

Hundreds of millions will be moving to cities like Shanghai to strike it rich and escape the rural life as more and more of the world's population continues the shift that's been going on, in fits and starts, since the Industrial Revolution: moving from the rural to the urban. By 1950, 30 percent of the world's population lived in cities. In 2000 this portion grew to 47 percent, and the United Nations predicts it will rise to 60 percent by 2030.[1] These would-be city dwellers want economic opportunities and material comforts that we take for granted: cell phones (and decent service), personal computers, access to private transportation, and household air conditioning.

Given this search for the good life and the amenities that go with it, the move toward urban life makes sense. Cities are capitalism's growth engine, offering opportunity along every dimension from finding a job to support oneself, to finding a mate to spend money on, to great cultural events to attend, to fantastic restaurants of all kinds. And, maybe, a bit later, parks to take the kids to. City growth has lifted billions of people out of poverty.

That's a good thing, although many lament the loss of agricultural and pastoral life. But how many of the those who bemoan the loss of farm living have gotten up before sunrise to milk cows by hand or slop pigs or pitch hay? I haven't, but I'm pretty sure it wouldn't be much fun, day after day. If you don't believe me, contrast Seinfeld's life in New York City with the cheery world of the Swiss Family Robinson.

Prominent writers such as Jared Diamond, author of the best sellers *Guns, Germs, and Steel* and the more foreboding

*Collapse*, are deeply worried about the environmental consequences of the growth of the middle class in the developing
world. Diamond, and most environmentalists, charge capitalism with causing climate change because urban growth
provides us with the income to afford a Hummer and a big
house. Capitalist growth, they say, perpetuates itself with an
advertising- and consumer-oriented culture ("The American
Dream") that manipulates our desires to consume more and
more carbon-intensive stuff: lawnmowers, air conditioners,
cars, car seats, disposable diapers, See 'n' Says (kids' products
produce a lot of carbon), and so on. Recent macroeconomic
trends support some of these claims. The world's population,
per capita income, and greenhouse gas emissions are all rising.
The world's population will have grown from 2.6 billion in
1950 to 6.9 billion by 2010.[2] Real-world per capita income is
now at $7,400, a figure that has grown sharply over the last
forty years. In 2005 the world produced 28.1 billion metric
tons of carbon dioxide; that number is predicted to rise to
42.3 billion metric tons per year by 2030.[3]

That's a lot of $CO_2$. Leading climate change researchers
have concluded that to protect the planet from potentially
catastrophic climate change risk, we must stabilize atmospheric carbon dioxide concentration at 500 parts per million
(ppm) or even as low as 350 ppm. But this would require reducing our total global carbon dioxide emissions to no more
than 19.1 billion tons per year—a little less than half of what's
predicted for 2030. In a world with 7 billion people—the
world's current population—we would have to shrink carbon

emissions to an average of about two and one-half tons per person per year. To put this in perspective, a car that gets about 25 miles to the gallon—a Toyota Corolla, which happens to be the most popular car in the United States—would exceed the 2.5-ton target at 7,500 miles per year (the average driver travels something like 12,000 miles a year). But driving is not our sole source of greenhouse gas emissions. When we turn on the lights, eat a steak, order a coffee, take a shower, send an e-mail, and do countless other little things during the day, they all result in extra greenhouse gas emissions.

Are you ready to cut back? If so, are you willing to cut back that much? If you answered "yes," you're probably kidding yourself. Evidence shows that very few individuals have cut back on their carbon-producing activities at all. Most of us are "free riders," hoping someone else will do the heavy lifting so we don't have to. The fundamental free rider problem is that each of us hopes that everyone else will cut back and allow us to keep "Hummering" (or Corolla-ing) along. Which is to say that attempts to reduce or reverse our carbon output—to mitigate the damage that we've already done—aren't going so well.

We're a bit like the *Titanic* on the night of April 14, 1912. We know how the *Titanic*'s story ends, but suppose the ship's watchman had seen the iceberg out in the distance. Anticipating that bad things happen when a ship hits such a big piece of ice, he would have issued a warning to the navigator to change course, and the disaster would have been averted.

Climate change and hitting an iceberg are different events, to be sure. In the case of the iceberg, the consequences of the ship hitting the ice are obvious and immediate. No Rush Limbaugh could step in and say that angry liberals are the real source of the problem. All aboard the *Titanic* would agree that they have a huge problem if they hit the iceberg. Nobody on board would say, "Well, that will only hurt the people in third class, and I never liked them anyway." The *Titanic* did not have enough lifeboats for everyone. Even the rich could not be sure that they would escape alive if a collision took place. Once those on board the *Titanic* spotted the iceberg, everyone would agree that switching direction to avoid it would be a wise move. The crew and passengers would know they would immediately be victims and all go down together. In contrast, as climate scientists demand that we take costly action to reduce global carbon concentrations to as low as 350 ppm, many people do not see why we should do so, even though we can see the iceberg.

We know what the future, our iceberg, looks like, almost guaranteed: more people, more money per person, and more overall pollution. And that's our starting point in this book: we have already released too much greenhouse gas, and I see no credible signs that global emissions will decline in the near or medium future. Although the carbon mitigation agenda—the plan to reduce our emissions—is a worthy goal, we are unlikely to invent a magical new clean technology that allows us to live well without producing greenhouse gases. We are equally unlikely to devise a geo-engineering technological fix that vacuums up the world's existing carbon emissions. That is, unlike a ship, we can't turn away.

So if the world is going to get hotter, and more of the world's population is going to be living in cities, then the fundamental question is what the future of our cities will be in our hotter world. Some claim that our future is bleak. The 2008 Nobel laureate in economics, Paul Krugman, for instance, has argued that we are like a frog in a pot of slowly heating water, patiently waiting to be cooked when it comes to a boil.[4] He laments that although he knows the climate pot is getting hot, we frogs are blissfully ignorant of the coming doom that climate change will cause. It's worth noting, though, that frogs do actually jump out of heating water. They don't sit around waiting to get cooked. And neither will we.

I'm optimistic about the quality of our lives in the cities of the future, despite the very different climate conditions that we'll face. Urban life will go on in our hotter world. At the heart of my belief that we frogs won't cook is our individual freedom of choice, not to mitigate but to adapt. Unlike birds and butterflies, we have a much wider variety of choices and options that allow us to protect ourselves from climate change. This personal freedom opens up pathways that will greatly help urbanites cope with it. As climate change unfolds, billions of households will seek out strategies for protecting their families from harm. Some will move to higher ground to areas that are unlikely to flood; others will seek out products ranging from more energy-efficient air conditioning to higher quality building materials to protect themselves from climate change's blows.

My vision—that we will save ourselves by adapting to our ever-changing circumstances—stands in sharp contrast to the usual Hollywood theme of a singular hero such as Arnold or Harrison or even Sly saving us from Armageddon. Of course a bunch of people acting rationally in response to a slowly changing world wouldn't make for a really action-packed thriller. We're not all on board one big ship that we can save through one collective decision. Instead, we'll be "saved" by a multitude of self-interested people armed only with their wits and access to capitalist markets. In that way, my core theme is ironic: Capitalist growth created the problem of mass greenhouse gases, but now capitalism's dynamism and its ability to reinvent itself will help us to adapt to the climate changes we have created.

So how will this work? Over the last twenty years, I have lived in Chicago, New York City, Boston, and Los Angeles. While I sought out good job opportunities and the possibility of living in the same city as my wife, I also always sought cities that I thought offered a high quality of life. Put bluntly, I won't move to a city that doesn't have "it"—and I'm not alone. Cities compete with one another, although we don't normally think of them as doing so unless they're vying to host the Olympic Games. But they do. Climate change will affect the competitive landscape for cities, and people will be able to choose the winner by "voting with their feet." Around the world, cities are starting from different points in the race to adapt to climate change. Salt Lake City cannot flood. New York City can. Moscow is unlikely to suffer from extreme heat waves. Phoenix will. The geographical location of cities helps to define the diverse challenges they will face. Part of the challenge in predicting how cities will adapt to change is recognizing the diversity of the cities that exist. Some are coastal, some are tropical, some are rich, and some are poor. Some are located in democracies, whereas others are in dictatorships. In this book I seek to explain how all of these factors will affect the quality of urban life in a hotter world.

As climate change heats up our cities, it will create enormous demand for new products to protect people. Households that continue to live in a hotter Phoenix will seek out new architectural designs for homes, windows, and more energy-efficient air conditioning to protect them from summer heat. This is just the tip of the iceberg. Such anticipated demand creates opportunities for green entrepreneurs to step in and innovate, as well as serious competition as they fight with one another for market share. In this competition to seize the adaptation market, many of these ideas will fall flat, but the next "Green Google" is sure to emerge. Such efforts strengthen our cumulative ability to withstand climate change. Some worry that the resource scarcity caused by climate change will lead to war, but it's equally likely—and I believe more so—that the common risks we face will foster innovation that will protect us all. Once these new products are developed, they'll be relatively easy to mass produce and sell around the world. The technologies that emerge can be diffused worldwide. Whether it's Twitter, or solar panels, or the Tesla electric vehicle, the innovative capitalist culture will allow us to make a Houdini-style escape from climate change's most devastating impacts.

Describing our environmental future is risky business. In 1968 Paul Ehrlich famously predicted in his best seller *Population Bomb* that mass starvation would occur in the 1980s. He was wrong. At a lecture he gave at Stanford University, I heard him explain that his predictions did not come true because people read his book and adapted, and thus were able to avert disaster.[5]

I don't harbor the illusion that so many people will read this book that it will shift the course of history. But then, they don't need to. My economics training has taught me the role that expectations and incentives play in changing people's behavior. If we can get those right, we don't have to worry about doomsday scenarios, because we will adapt.

I recognize that my optimism may be viewed as audacious given our collective sleepy efforts to tackle (and in some cases even to acknowledge) climate change up to this point. During this time of war and economic uncertainty, climate change adaptation is a back burner issue. Despite Al Gore's efforts and futuristic Hollywood movies sketching our scary future (e.g., *The Day After Tomorrow*, which showed the entire world simultaneously flooding and freezing—but don't worry, Dennis Quaid saved the remnants of humanity), we are off to a slow start in preparing for the coming climate change. There are several possible explanations for this. First, we may be skeptics who like to laugh at Chicken Littles who announce that the sky is falling. We need to see climate change to believe it. Al Gore's PowerPoint show may not be sufficient truth; a few hot summers may not be sufficient proof. Second, we may anticipate the threat but be technological optimists who trust our nerdy engineers to dream up some technological geo-engineering fix if and when the time comes. Third, we may be impatient and lacking in imagination. Although we love our grandchildren, we think back to our grandparents and realize how much better our standard of living has been relative to theirs. We can foresee a similar generational progress for our grandkids (perhaps they will hop a space shuttle to Mars?).

In the case of climate change, there are huge uncertainties about what the climate consequences of filling the atmosphere with greater carbon levels are. Such atmospheric carbon concentrations could cause horrific temperature changes. The probability of these events is not small. Put bluntly, if the world's greenhouse gas emissions continue to rise to a level of 600 ppm, there is a non-negligible chance that the world's average temperature would increase 10 degrees Fahrenheit! There could be an abrupt melting of Greenland's ice sheet and a collapse of the West Antarctic ice sheet. These events would have a dramatic impact on sea level.

But we do know that we don't know for sure what these consequences will be. How do we respond to such known "unknowns"? There are two schools of thought in modern economics. The rising school of behavioral economists view us as a group of belly-scratching Homer Simpsons who, like the frog in the hot pot, simply say "D'oh!" Behavioral economists have a fundamentally pessimistic view of humans as lazy and myopic and unwilling to sacrifice for their long-term good. Whereas traditional economic man was a cold, calculating, self-interested individual (think of Mr. Spock from *Star Trek*), the new economic man is emotional, distracted, and sometimes illogical (think of Dr. McCoy). In a recent review in *The New Yorker* of two books written by behavioral scholars, Elizabeth Kolbert celebrated this "refreshing" change in the zeitgeist of modern economic research: "Who wants a friend or a lover who is too precise a calculator?"[6] (This quote may explain why so many economists, like me, marry other economists.)

In contrast, neoclassical economists view people as forward looking and willing to make choices today in response to anticipated threats. Such "rational expectations" in the face of known unknowns push the population to take proactive steps. The awareness of scary future scenarios provides the "rational man" with a head start in coping with climate change. For generations University of Chicago economists, from Nobel Laureate Milton Friedman to his student, Nobel Laureate Gary Becker, to his non–Nobel laureate student (me), have believed that people respond to incentives as they pursue their life goals. Individuals have every incentive to recognize when they are in an unfamiliar situation. In this case, we will invest in better information that helps to reduce the uncertainty. As our climate scientists learn more and more about the challenges we face, this information provides us with an early warning system, signaling us about what lies ahead. This information helps us to cope with change.

Returning to the frog in the hot pot analogy, suppose that Al Gore and Homer Simpson are both offered the opportunity to buy a home at a low price in an area that climate change scientists believe is at high risk for serious flooding. The Al Gores would either say no thanks, or if they accepted this offer, would take steps such as elevating the home and other costly flood-proofing actions to protect it. Homer would be blissfully unaware and would seize the purchase opportunity. Such complacent households may actually migrate away from "safe cities" such as Salt Lake City to risky beautiful cities such as New York City, if they trust government and engineers to invent a credible protection strategy. As more of these households move to such cities, their political clout increases, and they attract even more federal government funds for protection. Once such households have made their locational decisions and chosen what types of homes to live in, Mother Nature will either create a nasty flood or not. There is a high probability that no storm will take place (even in the face of climate change). In this case, Homer Simpson will live on as a happy man. If a terrible flood does take place, Homer will suffer, and Al Gore will not. A Darwinist would say that the Al Gores will have to repopulate the planet after the days of reckoning begin.

But don't count out Homer. Forward-looking entrepreneurs, who smell the profits they can earn off the desperate Homers, will be ready with a variety of products to help the Homers cope with their new reality. At the end of the day, the story will have a happy ending. Some urban places suffer, but urbanites continue. In a very different context, Winston Churchill said, "Never in the field of human conflict was so much owed by so many to so few."[7] That quote also applies in the case of climate adaptation. A small cadre of forward-looking entrepreneurs will be ready to get rich selling the next generation of products that will help us all to adapt.

It has happened before. Whenever we humans have been confronted by disasters, we have recovered—even from some really big ones. Chapter 2 discusses some of these events and the lessons we can learn from them, which we can apply to living in our hotter future.

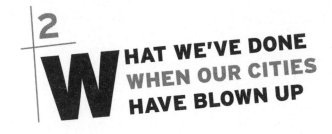

# 2

## WHAT WE'VE DONE WHEN OUR CITIES HAVE BLOWN UP

**Roughly 74,000 years** ago an enormous volcano near Sumatra erupted with a force a thousand times that of the 1980 eruption of Mount Saint Helens.[1] The ash that filled the sky blocked the sun's rays and is believed to have sharply lowered global temperatures. Granted, we didn't live in cities 74,000 years ago, but the drop in temperature—estimated to be 3 degrees Celsius—caused countless human deaths.[2] Just a few thousand families survived. Since then we have clearly made quite a comeback. In fact, the disaster may account for our species' success. Neurophysiologist William Calvin argues that modern human cognition, including sophisticated language and the capacity to plan ahead, springs from this disaster. The way we think—what, according to some, defines us as human—evolved in response to the demands of this long age of turbulence.[3] So maybe there's hope for us yet.

Since we started settling in cities about 12,000 years ago (according to the archaeological evidence, the oldest site of permanent human settlement is probably Damascus, Syria), we have been subject to lots of shocks, both locally and globally. Our cities have been bombed, burned, infected, quaked, razed, and flooded. For our purposes—figuring out how we're going to respond to the slow disaster that we're participating in right now—that's good news. This litany of doom and gloom offers a type of laboratory for studying how cities recover from disaster, and how we might respond as the earth gets hotter, and, equally important, what we probably shouldn't do.

In the aftermath of horrible shocks, many (but not all) cities have recovered quickly. In some cases, such as New York City after the 9/11 terrorist attacks, the city's productive and lifestyle advantages outweighed the short-term pain caused by the recovery process. In other cases, such as post-Katrina New Orleans, the government has stepped in with massive assistance reminiscent of the Marshall Plan that helped rebuild Europe after World War II. Of course, climate change doesn't have an exact correspondence with any past disaster. Many of the disasters discussed in this chapter were quite literally shocks, events that struck a particular city out of the blue and then dissipated (even in the case of long-term effects, like those of the flooding of New Orleans). But, that said, we can still learn valuable lessons that are relevant for thinking ahead to how our cities will cope with climate change's future shocks.

## Lesson 1: Destruction Often Triggers a Boom

The Chicago Fire of 1871 destroyed 2,124 acres and 17,450 buildings, killed 300 people, and left 99,000 people homeless. Yet ten years after the fire, the *New York Times* reported,

> buildings have been erected of three times the value of those destroyed and in this connection it must be borne in mind that the old Chicago was largely composed of wooden buildings, while the new is all brick, stone, or iron. The buildings, too, are larger, and represent a much larger capacity than would the same number of the old style. In this decade, the population has increased from 298,000 to 503,000. Business has kept apace with the increase in buildings and population, and it is true that Chicago never was so great and prosperous as to-day, and, although it is the anniversary of a calamity, all may take pride in their city.[4]

There are two ways to interpret these facts. First, it could be a case study of what economist Joseph Schumpeter called "creative destruction." The destruction of the old, low-quality building stock created a demand to rethink and rebuild the city. An alternative explanation is that Chicago was booming despite the nasty fire. The only way we could figure out whether the shock *caused* the boom is to find another Chicago (circa 1871) and watch its growth trajectory if the fire had not taken place.

As you might suppose, either finding an exact replica of 1871 Chicago and then watching it grow, or going back in time to 1871 and preventing the fire, though fodder for a passable science fiction novel, is beyond the power of mere economists. Not only can economists not travel back through time, we're also not allowed to run experiments in which a random subset of cities is burned or bombed (the treatment) while another set of randomly chosen but similar cities is not, so we can observe under what conditions cities recover.

Without the ability to run such an experiment, economists are forced to rely on studies in which we sit and wait for a volcano to explode (to test how air pollution affects health) or for a sex offender to move into a town (to measure how fear of crime affects local home prices) and then conduct a before and after comparison. Some economists have used this approach to study "fun" shocks like how people change their lives after winning the lottery (they are more likely to quit their jobs and divorce their spouses than are similar people who have not won the lottery).[5] Other economists have used the same methods to study the consequences of "serious" shocks such as assassinations. By comparing the aftermath of political outcomes across the world for nations in which assassinations succeeded and failed for all world leaders from

1875 to 2004, one set of economists documented that successful assassinations of autocrats produced sustained moves toward democracy.[6] This approach can also be applied to studying how major cities have coped with significant tragedy.

History provides the perspicacious researcher with opportunities to figure out just how similar cities respond to being bombed. The relevant question here is how quickly the bombed cities caught up to the cities that were spared—if they did at all. Bombings cause large amounts of damage in physically well-defined areas, so economists can look at the cities that were bombed, and then compare the growth rates of the bombed cities with one another as well as with nearby, similar cities that weren't bombed at all.

This is exactly what Donald Davis and David Weinstein, two Columbia University economists, did in a prominent study in 2002. Davis and Weinstein recognized that the Allies' wartime bombings of Japanese cities offer exactly the laboratory necessary for testing how cities recover. They studied population growth trends for Japanese cities that each had populations of more than 30,000 in 1925. Of this set of 303 cities, 66 were bombed during World War II. The bombing destroyed almost half of all structures in these cities—a total of 2.2 million buildings. Two-thirds of the cities' productive capacity vanished. Some 300,000 Japanese were killed. Forty percent of the population was rendered homeless. Counting all of the dead, missing, and displaced, some cities lost as much as half of their population.[7] In the nuclear bombings of Hiroshima, over two-thirds of the built-up area of the city was destroyed—covering more than 20 percent of the city's population. The second atomic weapon, dropped on Nagasaki, destroyed over 40 percent of the city's buildings.

These cities enjoyed an amazing postwar comeback. Davis and Weinstein measured "recovery" based on a city's population growth recorded at five-year intervals between 1925 and 1965. Population growth data indicate that people moved to the bombed cities, and survivors in these cities chose not to leave. This "voting with your feet" reveals that a city's economic opportunities and quality of life must be good (otherwise people would leave). Davis and Weinstein document that the average bombed Japanese city's population grew sharply within fifteen years following the end of World War II. Even the two cities (Hiroshima and Nagasaki) hit with nuclear bombs had been repopulated. By 1960 their population levels had recovered to what one might have guessed they would be had one only observed their population growth up until World War II, before they were bombed. Between 1945 and 1965 these cities made quite a comeback.

The case of Japan's cities is not a freak outlier. The population dynamics for German cities bombed during World War II reveal the same pattern. The Allies dropped tons of bombs on German cities such as Dresden. But Germany's bombed cities experienced relatively sharp population growth after the war. During the Vietnam War, the U.S. cumulative bombing represented one hundred times the combined impact of the Hiroshima and Nagasaki atomic bombs. A Berkeley research team who compared long-term impacts of the war in

584 Vietnamese districts that had faced very different bombing intensities found that despite this awesome firepower, there was no robust adverse impact of U.S. bombing on poverty rates, consumption levels, electricity infrastructure, literacy, or population density through 2002; that is, the U.S. bombs had little to no long-term impact on the growth of Vietnamese cities.[8] This isn't to say that bombing cities is a good idea, but the common theme of these three case studies is that bombed cities and areas recover, and relatively quickly, without suffering long-term consequences.

There is no law of physics requiring that a city that has experienced a shock *must* fully recover. Just look at upstate New York. Whenever there is an open election to be the governor or a senator from New York State, important politicians such as Hilary Clinton go on a "listening tour" upstate. These politicians see firsthand this area's economic hardship. Formerly booming cities along the Erie Canal in Upper New York State such as Buffalo, Syracuse, Utica, Rochester, and Troy have suffered from the exodus of corporate headquarters and the migration of manufacturing to China and the non–union friendly Southern states. Although the economic shocks these cities have experienced are less dramatic than a bombing, the exodus of jobs has taken a larger toll in the long run. Each of these cities experienced its peak population between 1930 and 1950 and has experienced over a 30 percent reduction in population since then. Although the jobs have left these cities, a sturdy housing stock built for a previous booming age lives on. The long-lived durability of the housing stock means that households can live cheaply in this area. A Manhattanite is not used to being able to buy a home for $55,000, but Troy offers homes at this price.[9]

## Lesson 2: A Federal Government "Jump Start" Is Not a Free Lunch

Hurricane Katrina, which struck in August 2005, has certainly accelerated the migration of people away from New Orleans, although the city was already in decline. The city's population has shrunk from 627,000 in 1960 to 485,000 in 2000 to 311,000 in 2008.[10]

Since Katrina, the federal government has invested more than $120 billion in the region.[11] To appreciate how big a number that is, compare it to the post–World War II Marshall Plan, General George Marshall's program for rebuilding Western Europe.[12] Marshall spent $13 billion—the equivalent of $126 billion in current dollars—to help over 140 million people in Western Europe in 1950. We have now spent an equal amount on the New Orleans general region to help far fewer people.[13]

The media have played a key role in focusing attention on New Orleans. The *New York Times* has mentioned "Hurricane Katrina" in more than 3,000 articles since 2005, 899 mentions in the last two years alone. This is just the tip of the iceberg in terms of media coverage. Who knows how many hours of television have been devoted to Katrina coverage?[14]

The media play a key role in determining which daily events are "shocking disasters." After all, in a world with 7 billion people, something potentially shocking takes place every day, but somehow only a small number of events actually galvanize us. The people of the United States are likely to be more generous with their time and money if they see the devastation caused by the disaster. Alternatively, if they do not experience the damage in some way, they are more likely to take the "out of sight, out of mind" approach.

Thomas Eisensee and David Strömberg document just how distractible the U.S. public is. They studied the influence of mass media on U.S. government response to approximately 5,000 natural disasters occurring between 1968 and 2002. These disasters took an average of 63,000 lives and affected 125 million people, per year. They showed that U.S. relief efforts depend on whether the disaster occurs at the same time as other newsworthy events, such as the Olympic Games. The explanation for this is that during the Olympics, the public is not paying attention to the disaster because they are watching the games. A disaster generates much less awareness and sympathy when the public is distracted.[15] This suggests that in the near future when many cities will be simultaneously suffering from climate blows, the general public will not have the time or interest to simultaneously follow all of these stories and to be generous. The New Orleans case may be the anomaly in terms of the amount of federal money it has received.

Federal investments in rebuilding a city do attract private-sector investment. A plausible chain of events is that a disaster occurs, the media fixate on it, the government responds, and then the private sector piggybacks on the opportunities offered by the government's "big push." The federal government's quick infusion of money acts as a stimulus that accelerates the rebuilding process. When billions of dollars of federal money flow into the destroyed area, construction workers and firms salivate at the opportunities. Disasters do cause state per capita income growth as new economic activity takes place to replace what has been destroyed.

It is unknown whether similar private-sector money would have flowed in if the federal government had not offered a dime. Again, we can't go back in time and run an experiment in which the federal government chooses a hands-off approach after Katrina. Would Goldman Sachs have viewed New Orleans as a high return investment? Its cold hearted bankers might have said to themselves, "This place is a swamp and this storm indicates what could happen again in the future. This is too risky; let's invest somewhere else."

One could make a case for compensating the storm's victims out of fairness and compassion, but it's much harder to make the case from a business standpoint. In contrast, when productive areas in locations where people want to live are damaged, strong market forces encourage these areas to rebuild. The destroyed area has great potential due to both its productivity and its inherent quality-of-life opportunities.

But the federal government isn't taking the cold-hearted business approach. It jumps in to provide disaster relief because the public—driven by news stories of suffering and devastation, of people and small, fuzzy pets trapped, with pictures of old ladies on their roofs—wants it to. The nation wants to help, and the nation acts through the federal government (and individuals act through charitable donations). The federal government might also worry about refugees. If the area is not rebuilt, then tens of thousands of people might migrate to nearby cities and disrupt day-to-day life. Consider, for instance, how refugees from New Orleans put inordinate burdens on cities like Houston and Atlanta. On the other hand, federal intervention represents a transfer of money from all of the nation's taxpayers to the victims.[16]

A second justification for massive government intervention is the belief that the free market would take too long on its own to repair a city. The famous British economist John Maynard Keynes said, "In the long run we are all dead." He was using his wit to push back against the conventional wisdom of free market economists (such as myself) that the free market economy could quickly respond and adjust to any unexpected shock (such as the Great Depression). A market solution to a disaster would look something like this: The natural disaster shock destroys valuable capital such as homes and buildings. This triggers demand to replace these lost structures. Using money from private insurance policies, construction crews are hired to rebuild what was lost. This increase in demand creates new job opportunities and drives up wages in the city; this helps to jump-start the next boom.

Subsequent generations of Keynesians have consistently argued that the "short-run" period of unemployment and idle resources often turns out to be not so short. Some workers, especially those who are older and less educated, face high migration costs for moving to other cities offering economic opportunities. If such workers are stuck in cities with no good job prospects, they could be unemployed for a long time. Some economists argue that, adding insult to injury, the experience of unemployment scars. Put simply, unemployment is not a welcome vacation. Some may respond to losing their jobs by drinking booze, not bathing, and sleeping in. Such a "glamorous" new lifestyle could make one less employable in the future. The experience of being unemployed could cause people to be more likely to be unemployed in the future.

With these concerns in mind, Keynes advocated that governments run deep deficits during bad times to help jump-start the economy. He suggested—and he was only half kidding—that the government put money in bottles, bury them, and have the unemployed go look for the treasure. This scheme would redistribute income, which could quell any incipient revolution by the poor and give them newly found purchasing power to increase consumer spending. This in turn would stimulate new production that would create jobs and in aggregate the capitalist economy would start to roar again.

But a Keynesian local "big push" to rebuild a city is not a free lunch. The federal government must raise taxes on everyone else, raise future taxes, or cut other spending to pay for this localized expenditure. The money has to come from somewhere. High taxes come with all sorts of problems. For instance, economies with high taxes will feature more black market activity (people will want to be paid in cash that they do not report to the tax authorities). High taxes also affect capital accumulation and work effort (because taxes lower after-tax wages, this encourages people to work less and take more leisure). The net effect of taxes encouraging less savings and work effort is a poorer nation—even if the damaged city is growing more quickly as a result.

A resident of Albany, New York, might wonder why his taxes are going up to rebuild part of the New Orleans coast. He might say to himself, "I understand why my tax dollars go to pay for the military and to pay for unemployment insurance—those help everyone—but why do I have to pay to rebuild New Orleans after a hurricane hits? How does that benefit me? Why can't the coastal cities tax themselves and pay for their own defense?" These are all good questions.

## Lesson 3: Government Activism Can Put More People at Risk

S trangely, government action can also actually put more people at risk. In 1993, a major flood in Missouri, where the Mississippi, Illinois, and Missouri rivers meet, caused roughly $15 billion of damage and fifty deaths.[17] Tens of thousands of people were evacuated. At least 10,000 homes were totally destroyed, and hundreds of towns were hit hard, with at least seventy-five towns completely under flood waters.[18] And yet today, more than $2.2 billion worth of new development in the St. Louis area stands on land that was under water during the 1993 flood.[19] Between 1993 and 2003, offices, shopping centers, and highways covered at least 4,200 acres of Missouri flood plain, most of which were under water during the 1993 flood. Why so much development? The federal government, both through disaster relief and by providing flood insurance, has reduced risk to the point where developers felt comfortable building in a zone that is really unsafe. The building boom did bring jobs, services, and tax revenue to the region, but it could lead to more damage in future floods.

Encouraging development in a flood plain is risky—but that's exactly what the federal government's well-intentioned actions did. And climate change will make it even riskier.

Why would any company want to develop flood-prone land in the first place? The answer is a phenomenon called a "land assembly problem." Developers hoping to build a new hotel complex or mall need parcels of land that are big enough to build on, but it's difficult to find a large plot of land with nothing on it that is in a desirable location. Most available urban lots are smaller and not next to each other. Think of a chess board. If you own the black squares, you need to buy the white squares to have the necessary land to build a hotel. If the current owners of the white squares will not sell to you, then you cannot build your development.

Large lots are available in the flood zone, and developers and the government are well aware of this. The developers smell new profits from the commercial opportunities offered by building and managing hotels and malls. The local government is excited about the new tax revenue, construction jobs, and full-time jobs once the complex is built. As time passes after a big flood, it is human nature to dismiss the likelihood of suffering a new nasty shock—like fresh flooding.

Although laughing off a flood in a flood zone may be wishful thinking, risk perception is heavily shaped by recent events. After the terrorist attacks of 9/11/2001, for example, I was afraid to fly. Although objectively the sharp increase in airport security had made flying safer, I was not able to forget the recent events. But over time, without a repeat of the events of that morning, I, like many others, discounted the possibility of a 9/11-like event and now fly all the time. In the case of climate change–related shocks, climate scientists face the awkward challenge of warning people about the new risks an area such as St. Louis faces without being branded a Chicken Little, forever crying that the sky is falling.

Government policy has played an important role in encouraging economic development in risky parts of St. Louis and other flood zones. Much of the commercial and residential development is in levee-protected areas, where flood insurance is not required. Taxpayers (which is to say everyone) subsidize flood plain development through levee construction, levee repair, disaster aid, insurance costs, and infrastructure such as roads, bridges, and drainage systems. Some of the money for levee protection is provided by local bond measures; other money comes from the federal government.[20] An unintended consequence of using federal money is that these defensive investments encourage development in the risky area. In Missouri about 75 percent of recent development has taken place on land that was under water in 1993.[21] Climate change is likely to increase the risk of future flooding in such areas.

The tough job is to figure out rules that encourage growth while simultaneously giving businesses the right incentives to locate in relatively safe areas and to invest in materials that can withstand a nasty flood. Professional geographers have made great progress creating high-quality maps, which can be used for many purposes. Parcel-by-parcel mapping capability now allows us to pinpoint small plots of land that are and are not at high flood risk. My UCLA colleagues John Agnew and Tom Gillespie made the national news when they used their maps to make pinpoint predictions concerning where Osama bin Laden must have been hiding near the Pakistan border.[22] I don't believe that they have collected the $25-million reward for helping the U.S. government hunt down bin Laden but I respect their initiative and their study does highlight how using multiple pieces of geographical data can be used to solve practical problems. (Products like Google Earth also allow one to look at one's home or childhood house from a bird's eye view. Although my son was not impressed to see my childhood house, I was!)

Using current mapping capabilities, one can overlay maps of flood zones on top of zoning parcel maps, yielding a map that could be used to identify parcels of land to develop that are at low risk for flooding. Those parcels that face higher flood risk should cost more to insure. Critics might call this "discrimination" or "price gouging," but it would force firms to take a hard look at the consequences of where they are considering locating.

Right now, government policy is allowing businesses in the St. Louis region to flip a one-sided coin. If no flood occurs, then the investment in developing in the flood zone was a wise move. If a disaster does take place, the region's congressional representatives and senators will claim that their constituents are the victims of horrible luck, are suffering, and need federal disaster money. But are they really victims?

Consider another set of victims—namely, the set of people who go to Las Vegas and bet on the losing Super Bowl team. Nobody feels sorry for the Las Vegas "losers," but many of us do feel sorry for the "victims" who built their hotel in the flood plain. If the Super Bowl betters all lived in Idaho, could they go to their senator to get their money back from the federal government? I view the Missouri hotel owners and the Super Bowl betters as equal gamblers. One may say that the Missouri businessmen were unaware of the risks. But their job is to factor in all risks before making a costly decision, and they could have hired climate forecasters as consultants before they built their hotels—just as the Las Vegas gamblers could have consulted odds makers before they put their cash on the barrelhead.

The anticipation of government protection that comes after the fact creates incentives to take dangerous risks. A libertarian like the economist Milton Friedman would offer no government money to rebuild damaged cities, a move that would short-circuit the current system. Without any guarantee of a government bailout, developers would have to think long and hard and really understand the risks they face before committing to building in a flood plain—no matter how big the parcels might be. Such a government stance would mean that individuals would know that they have to protect themselves. This "tough love" economist's policy would encourage more people to move away from at-risk areas or at least use better materials in building homes in at-risk areas. If the federal government is serious about pushing cities and states to adapt to climate change, then it must think through the unintended consequences of its current policies.

The hotel industry and the government are playing a type of game. The hotel industry's thinking when building a nice hotel along a coastline is that, "If the government builds the coastal protection, then our investment will be safe and this pretty hotel will generate a lot of revenue." The government says to itself, "Projects such as sea walls are supposed to pass a cost/benefit test. We know what it costs to build these sea walls but the benefits of this project hinge on what physical assets (i.e. buildings) and lives are protected by our project. If a hotel will be built here, then the benefits of our building the sea wall are larger because we are protecting more lives and the capital stock." After all, it wouldn't make sense to build a sea wall if nobody lives in the city.

The irony here is that the government's willingness to build the sea wall actually *increases* the population's climate change risk exposure. At first glance it is obvious that government investment in sea walls and infrastructure makes *urban places* safer. St. Louis or New Orleans would suffer less flooding with better antiflooding infrastructure. But more people and more investment will flow into a city that is perceived to be safe. If these people would have moved to a climate-safe city such as Salt Lake City in the absence of such government investments then the government's actions have *caused* more climate risk exposure.

### Lesson 4: What Doesn't Kill Us Makes Us Stronger

In the aftermath of recent hurricanes, Florida has sharply ramped up its new building codes, which has led to higher-quality real estate stock. In Florida, owners of homes built after 1996 are much less likely to file insurance claims than owners of homes built before 1996.[23] This abrupt decline in filings is due to stronger regulatory codes. The net result is that future hurricanes will cause less damage to Florida's housing stock because regulation has forced the stock to be built to a higher level of quality. If a government states that engineering improvements are needed, this technology forcing and standard setting provides a strong incentive for engineers to focus their efforts. The net effect of such efforts is an improvement in infrastructure quality and less damage. The market values these quality improvements. Consider the effect of the stricter 1994 South Florida Building Codes on local home prices. Homes built under the stricter code sold for about 10 percent more, on average, than comparable homes built under the old code.[24]

Other cities around the world can learn from Florida about what types of building codes are cost effective for reducing hurricane damage. As home builders practice working with materials for constructing "hurricane proof" homes, this knowledge can be readily exported to other nations to help them prepare for expected blows. In this Internet age, best practices discovered by one city will quickly diffuse around the globe.

Natural disasters not only lead to a re-evaluation of regulatory codes, they also push architects to think about how to build the next generation of homes.[25] Hurricane Katrina would have caused less damage if the flooded homes had been able to float on the flood water. To address this issue, UCLA architect Thom Mayne has designed the FLOAT house in collaboration with Brad Pitt's Make It Right Foundation. The house has been described by a reporter for the *Seattle Times*:

> Called the FLOAT House, the unique home aims to answer the challenge posed by the Big Easy's flood risk. The home is long and narrow like the traditional New Orleans shotgun home and sits on a raised 4-foot base. The Morphosis floating house technology was developed and is in use in the Netherlands, where architects are working to address rising sea levels expected with climate change. In case of a flood, the base of the house acts as a raft, allowing the home to rise on guide posts up to 12 feet as water levels rise. While not intended for occupants to remain

inside during a hurricane, the structure is designed to minimize catastrophic damage and preserve the homeowner's investment. The floating home should also allow residents to return within days of a hurricane or flood.[26]

The architect hopes to mass market these homes, which he says can be produced for $150,000 each.

Thom Mayne is both a good architect and a good businessman. Anticipating that coastal areas such as New Orleans will continue to face residential building damage, he has worked for two years to develop a new product that can withstand anticipated shocks. Whether his motivation was altruism for flood victims or the self-interested pursuit of profit, his effort has yielded a new product that will reduce the cost of future floods.

His floating home's ability to improve quality of life in cities at risk from flooding hinges on whether homeowners will buy his product. If his home is seen as high quality, and if households fear that dangerous floods will become more frequent in the New Orleans area, then demand will increase. His association with Brad Pitt will not hurt! New products always face some skepticism. People have trouble imagining the benefits of owning a very new product because they have no experience with it. Mann would be wise to film a YouTube video of Brad Pitt conducting a tour of the new home. After the introduction of a new product (whether it is a plasma television, iPhone, or floating house), experience with the product can often increase demand.

From a marketing standpoint, the home's manufacturers should consider making a video of a simulated flood to demonstrate how this new product performs under such stressful circumstances. (Perhaps the video could star Brad Pitt and Angelina Jolie.) If a first generation of "guinea pigs" could convey (perhaps through blogging) their experience with the new product, this word-of-mouth learning would quickly spread.

### Lesson 5: Don't Forget the Little Guys

After the terrorist attacks of 9/11/2001, Mayor Rudy Giuliani was lauded for his strong leadership. His success as the man who led New York City out of the dark days of the terrorist attacks got him on the television show Saturday Night Live (where he told us it was OK to laugh again) and helped launch his bid for the Republican presidential nomination. After Hurricane Katrina, President George W. Bush faced intense criticism for not leading. These examples highlight that we have grown accustomed to having some "great man" step up and coordinate our concerns and responses to a tragedy and help lay out a master plan for recovery.

But the beauty of modern society is that we are not millions of ants being bossed around by the Queen Ant. In our decentralized society, there are roles for many of us to play in launching a comeback. History shows that there are many unknown heroes whose actions help to rebuild injured cities.

During the Great Chicago Fire of 1871, Potter Palmer, a prominent Chicago businessperson and founder of Potter Palmer and Company, lost to the fire his recently built Palmer House Hotel, as well as several of his other buildings on State Street. In order to rebuild, he obtained the largest loan issued to an individual at the time, for $1.7 million. Palmer also developed swampland to the north of Chicago's business district into Lake Shore Drive, which to this day is one of the wealthiest neighborhoods in Chicago.[27]

Arthur Ducat was a Chicago insurance underwriter who played an integral role in shaping Chicago's fire code policies after the 1871 fire. He and Frederick Baumann wrote one of the most detailed building law codes. Ducat's policies were later copied by other states and municipalities and remain influential to this day.[28]

After the 1906 San Francisco earthquake, panicked insurance policy owners ran to the Fireman's Insurance Company to collect on their policies. A major property and casualty insurer, particularly in San Francisco's commercial district, Fireman's faced more than $11 million in claims but had only $7 million in assets in the summer of 1906. The firm could have gone bankrupt, and thousands would not have collected on their policy payments. J. B. Levison, who headed the company's Marine Division and later was its president for two decades, persuaded policyholders to accept a payoff plan that gave a large measure of relief to customers in the wrecked city. "It offered to pay claimants 50 percent in cash in installments of 20 percent and 30 percent. The balance of their claims was to be paid in stock in the restructured Fireman's Fund. The company issued 16,000 shares valued at $150 each. That gave the company time to recover and, ultimately, thrive."[29]

In each of these cases, creativity and financial risk taking in the aftermath of a disaster helped the city recover. These three examples are just the tip of the iceberg. For a city to recover, millions of people must individually conclude that despite the recent tragedy, the opportunities and quality of life offered in that city are better than elsewhere. After the terrorist attacks of 9/11, I incorrectly predicted that Columbia University and New York University would have trouble recruiting and retaining faculty because academics from around the country would view New York City as a more risky city that was prone to more attacks. But New York thrived (partially due to the finance boom), and these leading universities even grew stronger. In a world where people differ in their expectations of the future, these universities are likely to attract leading scholars who are the most optimistic about the city's future. Why? A true "Chicken Little" (such as me) would have demanded too much "combat pay" to join the university, and the schools' deans would have canceled the negotiations and pursued someone else. In the aftermath of a disaster, if people move to the recovering city without being paid a "combat bonus" to do so, this suggests that the city's future is bright (or at least that some people think it is).

## Lesson 6: We Are Not All in the Same Boat

Urban disasters do not affect everyone in the city equally. After the terrorist attacks of 9/11, at least 3,000 people were killed in the Wall Street area of Manhattan, buildings were destroyed, and many families were deeply affected. But the New York City metropolitan area is home to roughly 20 million people. The losses from this disaster were most heavily borne by people who work in the financial district and the rescue crews who responded to the disaster. In the case of Hurricane Katrina, the elderly and poor black households were overrepresented among the victims.

These cases raise two politically incorrect issues. First, in cities that anticipate that shocks are likely but that different parts of the city face different risks, will the collective public agree on how much to invest in protecting the city? Without a common threat, those who anticipate they will be victims will want to cost share for the defense with those who know that they are unlikely to be victims. These "high-ground" households are unlikely to be willing to sacrifice in the name of protecting the greater good when they know that they are not at risk. Second, once a climate change–induced shock occurs, will the wealthy be willing to redistribute what they have to the losers from the shock? This is less likely to occur if the city is polarized and has little social capital (connections between neighbors and communities).

The divides that exist between groups who live within the same city can be clearly seen in the aftermath of Katrina. A hot button issue in New Orleans has been the debate over the future of low-lying, flood-ravaged neighborhoods. Should they be rebuilt or should they be turned into wetlands?[30] Scientists and most of the white population prefer the latter solution, whereas the residents of these neighborhoods prefer the former. Such wetlands could act as a natural barrier against future floods. Some people want to build there again and to not surrender to "Mother Nature," but scientists have argued that rebuilding there would position the city for "additional, Katrina-like disasters." A poll of voters by Tulane University and the nonprofit Democracy Corps found that 64 percent of white respondents agreed that "some areas of New Orleans destroyed by Hurricane Katrina should not be rebuilt as residential areas again." Of blacks polled, 74 percent disagreed with the statement.[31]

In the Katrina case, the diverse city residents have conflicting goals. The white wealthy residents want a healthy metropolitan area that signals to the rest of the nation that New Orleans is safe and secure. The African American communities in the Lower Ninth District want to re-create what was there despite the risks involved.

Suppose that it is true that climate change's impacts will be concentrated among the urban poor. After all, they are likely to live in communities that face greater risk from climate change and to have less access to market products such as cars to aid an escape and medical care if they have been afflicted. Such "targeted" disaster creates a collective action challenge.

If climate change adaptation is viewed as a poor person's problem, then it is unlikely to attract middle-class support. In contrast, some of the most prominent social programs in the United States, such as Social Security and Medicare, have been based on the premise that we all have a stake in everyone's survival. Although some implicit redistribution takes place (in the case of Social Security, Bill Gates will receive small retirement payouts relative to his contributions), everyone in society receives benefits from these programs. This solidifies public support for these programs.

When the losses from shocks are concentrated among groups who are not politically powerful, the majority will simply shrug. Although there certainly are some altruistic people, the average person will not be willing to sacrifice much of his or her own income to protect strangers.

## Lesson 7: People Migrate in Response to Shocks

Migration will play an important part in how different cities respond in a hotter world. Rugged individualism is a major theme in our culture. Whether it is Dirty Harry enforcing the law against the bad guys or Bruce Willis saving the day in *Die Hard*, smart individuals can take charge when goofy bureaucrats fail. If different levels of government fail to protect individuals from risks, households can always rely on their wits and "vote with their feet," migrating to cities and communities that feel safer and more welcoming in our hotter world.

Many environmentalists are worried that in the developing world, climate change will create a new class of people called "environmental refugees," who will migrate across national borders as they seek safer areas featuring the basic necessities of life. Although this popular literature has hinted that this shock-induced migration is bad, an alternative view is that such migration is crucial for reducing the costs we incur from any given shock.

Consider the case of the Mariel boatlift. In 1980 more than 124,000 Cubans showed up in Miami. Observers in Miami at the time of the boatlift noted the strain caused by the Mariel immigration. The homicide rate increased nearly 50 percent between 1979 and 1980.[32] If the people who already lived in Miami were forced to remain in the city, they would have suffered from the triple whammy of higher rents for houses, lower wages, and a reduced quality of life. Simple supply and demand logic tells us that this immigration influx will increase the local demand for housing (raising rents) at the same time that it increases labor supply (lowering local wages).

But Miamians didn't have to stay in Miami. As the immigrant population moved into Miami, many native Miami residents moved to other cities. As a result, Miami's wages fell less and apartment rents rose less than they would have if the incumbents had remained.[33] There was no central planner who said, "Let's move a bunch of native Miami residents so we can be sure Miami will not be crippled by this refugee influx." The people who moved from Miami to Atlanta were probably thinking of making this move before the shock occurred. The Cuban immigration, by starting to raise rents and lower wages, pushed this group to leave. One study concluded that rents for native households seeking apartments similar to those demanded by the new Cuban immigrants increased by 9 percent after their arrival, whereas the costs for the expensive apartments in Miami (which faced little Cuban demand) did not increase at all.[34]

The ability to "vote with your feet" and migrate to other cities acts as a type of insurance policy. This insurance paid off in the case of the Cuban immigration but it will be even more valuable for cities around the world in the face of climate change. Many nations have several large cities. The United States has hundreds of cities with populations of more than 250,000. Climate change will not have an equal impact on each of these cities. The ability to migrate protects urban people and is especially valuable if governments are unable or unwilling to protect the populace.

Think of a city's residents as rabbits and slugs. The quick-moving rabbits (a mixture of younger people, renters, and more educated people) protect the slow-moving slugs (homeowners and older workers) from unexpected shocks, although the protection is not intentional. If Miami has 3 million people and its population suddenly expands to 3.3 million people then only 10 percent of the population needs to leave for it to remain in balance. No social planner is needed to go door to door trying to identify the 300,000 people who are willing to leave. Instead, self-interested people who are aware of the rent and wage differences between cities will decide whether it is time for them to go. And they don't have to be consciously aware; they can just notice that things have gotten tight from month to month, and their relatives in Atlanta talk about how great things are there. The beauty of relying on market signals such as prices to urge households to consider changing their behavior is that we never suffer the heartbreak of making a one-hundred-year-old widow and her twenty cats move from her childhood home.

Relative to renters, homeowners face higher moving costs. But don't feel too bad for them: they were aware of this when they decided to buy homes and presumably took into account that one of the costs of ownership is that one loses flexibility in responding to new information about employment prospects or quality of life in a given city. Homeowners have made a large financial bet that the local economy and the quality of their city will improve. If they have bet wrong, they suffer less if there are rabbits in the city who can respond to the downturn by moving away.

This history lesson about the consequences of the Mariel boatlift is highly relevant for thinking about the consequences of climate change. Migration between cities in the face of climate change will help to protect urbanites. Extremely mobile renters will suffer little if their origin city is struck by climate shocks. The main losers will be the landowners in such cities, who will own a less-valuable asset as the shock to the city becomes common knowledge.

One theme that emerges from this chapter is that government policies can significantly increase the degree of climate-related risks that a population faces. Investments in antiflood infrastructure and public insurance pricing have created a nasty unintended consequence: more economic activity located in the exact areas a risk-averse climate scientist would say to avoid. In the aftermath of disasters such as Hurricane Katrina, there is a clear short-term role for activist government intervention. Only government has the resources and the political clout to coordinate dispersed resources and address an unexpected calamity when time is of the essence. But in the long term the market is going to do a much better job of coordinating and problem solving. Our past success with dealing with change provides a road map for how to deal with the expected and the unexpected that lies ahead.

This chapter has focused on bombings, floods, and fires. Climate change, in contrast to these abrupt events, will unfold less dramatically. Its impacts will be widely felt rather than focused on a few narrowly defined geographical areas. This last point is important, because, as we'll see in chapter

3, climate change is going to have different levels and kinds of impact on different cities. It will, in effect, remake the competitive landscape of cities. Keeping in mind the lessons of this chapter, let's take a look at how competition among cities might change in our hotter future.

# 3
# KING OF THE HILL

**W**hen the Yankees play the Red Sox, or the Patriots face the Giants in the Super Bowl, part of the tension, excitement, and fun is based on the long rivalry between New York City and Boston. From at least the time when the Red Sox traded Babe Ruth to the Yankees, people from Boston have lived in the shadow of New York City. As a resident of Boston for nine years, I know that I viewed it as New York's "little brother," but with an edge of having a greater cluster of excellent universities.

Today, which is the better city to live and work in? The answer doesn't simply determine mere boasting rights. In today's skills economy, the cities that can lure and retain those with such skills will boom. A city that can attract the next Google has a bright future. Today, coastal cities such as Boston and New York and warm winter, sunny cities are winning the competition. Losing cities such as Cleveland and Detroit are slowly decaying as the housing stock and industrial capacity that was built up during the manufacturing heydays of the 1950s slowly but surely rust away. Detroit's population has shrunk from 1.8 million in 1950 to 912,000 in 2008.

The same dynamics are playing out in Germany and England. Industrial, northern cities such as Manchester are shrinking at the same time that high-skill southern cities at London's fringe, such as Reading, are growing.

The point is, cities compete. They compete for resources, bragging rights, and most especially population. Cities have to provide the amenities—from safe streets to clean air—that attract new residents and keep the old ones. And those residents, or most of them, have the ability to vote with their feet. They can move across the country or to a new country—to wherever their skills will take them that seems appealing.

Our hotter future, though, will completely change the game. The future won't look like it does now—but then it never has. As University of Chicago economist Frank Knight wrote in 1921, "The existence of a problem of knowledge depends on the future being different from the past, while the possibility of a solution of the problem depends on the future being like the past."[1] Although Knight is unlikely to have pondered the issue of climate change almost ninety years ago, he did anticipate the fundamental challenge of predicting how we will individually and collectively cope in our hotter world.

More than 80 percent of Americans live in a city, and commuting costs force us to live and work in the same place. When choosing our favorite city, we face tradeoffs. An economist who loves to surf will have mixed feelings about joining the University of Chicago's faculty. Although she would be fortunate to join a great university, she might not find Lake Michigan's waves much of a challenge. In a nutshell, we seek out a city that simultaneously offers a great quality of life and good job prospects. Few cities offer both—but some offer neither. Facing the market price of housing in different cities and knowing your own priorities, you must choose what is best for you.

Climate change will shake up the quality-of-life rankings of cities as climate amenities shift and the risk of drought or flooding (or both) changes. Some of today's superstar cities, like Venice, Italy, will face significant new risks, while inland, northern cities such as Milan will not. Major coastal cities will have to wrestle with tough engineering and public health challenges. This chapter explains how the competitive landscape will shake out as things get hotter. At the end, I offer a sneak preview of the "Best Cities to Live In" rankings around the year 2100. Whether you should buy real estate in such cities today, I leave to you.

## The Current Menu of Destination Choices

Even though the Internet now gives us the ability to telecommute from a log cabin in the bucolic woods, most of us continue to want to live in cities. Cities help us to learn new skills and meet and trade with other people. There will always be a new generation of young people seeking to network and establish their reputations, looking for friends and romance and culture. There's a reason television shows such as *Seinfeld* and *Sex in the City* are set in New York City, not on the Kansas plains.

Urbanites have many choices of where to live. Whereas language barriers and cultural differences create psychological costs for moving within the European Union, within the United States there is relatively easy mobility across states and regions. Roughly 3 percent of Americans move to different states every year. The United States has sixty metropolitan areas with at least 900,000 people and 164 metropolitan areas with at least 250,000 people. Although all big cities have common features such as Starbucks and a downtown, these cities differ in any number of ways. Some are coastal; others are inland. Some are new cities built mainly after World War II, whereas others peaked fifty years ago. Some cities are hot during summer; others are cool. Some are known for their green beauty; others continue to have a legacy of past manufacturing, gritty, industrial/commercial real estate.

## The New, Hotter Playing Field?

Although climate change will not affect the quality of the football played in domed stadiums, like the New Orleans Superdome, it will change what day-to-day life is like in these cities. Low-probability, high-risk scenarios (e.g., massive floods) will also become more likely. Anticipating the challenges and opportunities that will arise will have major economic consequences. Over the next fifty years, hundreds of millions of new homes and countless new commercial buildings will be built. In our hotter world, where should they be built? Will major mega-cities emerge from what are today sleepy towns?

If Americans' sole goal is to survive in the face of climate change, then we could build new cities far from the coasts and close to the Canadian border, in states such as North Dakota. We have seen such sharp urban population growth before. In 1950 only 25,000 people lived in the city of Las Vegas. By 2008 the city had grown to 560,000, and more than 1.8 million people live in the greater metropolitan area. People who visit Las Vegas are amazed at how creative investment has transformed this moonscape. In Las Vegas are small-scale versions of New York City's Central Park and the Eiffel Tower. This could be a preview of what is to come. Although Vegas may not be "authentic," it does suggest the transplantation possibilities enabled by financial capital and some imagination. The current residents of North Dakota's cities, such as Fargo, might not be too happy about having loud-mouthed

New Yorkers moves in by the millions, but they would certainly be impressed with the cash that New Yorkers could offer for local land. Today, one can purchase an acre of land in Fargo for roughly $100,000.[2]

In truth, we will not be able to replicate New York's culture or San Francisco's tolerance in a "safe city" in our hotter world. Thus, each of us will face fundamental tradeoffs. We all seek an affordable, high-quality-of-life city, but a by-product of our individual attempts to pinpoint such a city means that it won't exist! Just as a Mercedes costs more than a Honda Accord, those cities with a high quality of life will feature higher home prices and offer relatively low wages. Each of us has a sense of what we consider to be the good life, and taking each city's strengths and weaknesses as given, we choose where we want to live our lives. This competition between cities exists because people can vote with their feet and migrate to other cities. Just as the Miamians did when the Cubans arrived, if they're really unhappy, people will pick up and move. Some cities (like Detroit) have lost badly. And some seem never to lose (like New York or Paris or Tokyo). But they do compete.

## The Super Bowl

The educated are highly mobile and are willing to move whenever they anticipate better opportunities. A city that wants to thrive should pay careful attention to whether skilled workers want to be there. After all, attracting and retaining the skilled is the key determinant of long-term city growth.[3] Cities used to compete for manufacturing gigs so they could have a nice, stable middle class, but they now compete for the "Google Guys."

The U.S. population is increasingly concentrated in the South and West. In 1900, 38 percent of the nation's population lived in these regions. By the year 2000, this percentage had grown to 58 percent. This regional migration has led to huge population growth in new cities such as Phoenix, Las Vegas, and Dallas and slow population growth in older, colder cities such as Buffalo and Cleveland.

Climate change will slow the growth of these new cities. Their summers will become too hot, and water is likely to become scarce. If households no longer want to live in such cities, employment growth will slow. In the modern economy, there are few industries that face geographic determinism; a Starbucks or a law firm can locate anywhere. At the end of the day, footloose skilled workers will want to work where they want to live. In the recent past, somebody who wanted to work in the car industry had to locate in Detroit. But today new auto makers such as Coda Automotive are headquartered in places like Santa Monica; Coda's bosses enjoy the sunshine and relatively easy access to flights to China, where the company's prototype electric vehicle is being mass produced.[4]

Major cities compete for good buzz; they want to avoid labels such as "Murder Capital of the United States" or "Smog Capital" or "Traffic Capital." In this age of the Internet and easy air travel, even the best public relations firms cannot trick the public into believing that a dirty, dangerous city is great. People are well informed about day-to-day life in various cities. They can read a local newspaper or blogs or call friends in that city. They can travel to that city and walk around in it before they actually move. Twitter offers continuous feeds of real-time information about current events.

Having real-time access to information about cities and their communities means that people will make better decisions about choosing the right neighborhood for them. As climate change unfolds, we will individually learn about the new opportunities and challenges of living in different cities. A humid city such as St. Louis may face a worse mosquito problem than before climate change unfolded. Bloggers will quickly report this "new news," and potential migrants will make informed decisions. This kind of full information will minimize migrants' regret and guarantee that high-quality-of-life cities will be in demand. As climate change hits, this information will be quite valuable in educating potential migrants to a city about the true challenges of living there.

## Urban Quality of Life

As mayor of New York City, Rudi Giuliani took great pride in claiming that his policies had restored law and order to this notoriously high-crime city. Whether this claim is true remains an open question, but the fact is that since the early 1990s, New York has enjoyed a sharp reduction in its violent crime rate. New York is now a much less risky place than it used to be. Recognizing this, people are more likely to enjoy the city's nightlife and take small lifestyle risks such as jogging in Central Park at night—which they may have avoided in the 1970s. Such salient shifts in the reality and perceptions of a city's "livability" can affect both the quality of life and the economic performance of a city. This is especially true as cities rely more and more on tourism as a growth industry.

But consider Pittsburgh in the 1950s or Manchester, England, in the 1870s, where heavy manufacturing was the golden goose, creating jobs and economic opportunity. In those days there was a fundamental tradeoff. The golden goose was quite dirty. Workers in these "satanic" cities sacrificed quality of life to receive a good paycheck. Today, cities have a strong economic incentive to preserve their reputation as green and clean.

Between 1951 and 2000, the number of manufacturing jobs in New York County, which is the center of the New York City metropolitan area, declined, from 1,082,188 to 146,291. That's a loss of almost one million jobs! Manufacturing accounted for 36 percent of the county's employment in 1951, compared to only 5.3 percent in 2000. On the other hand, between 1969 and 2000, service employment increased from 25.4 percent of the local economy to 41.1 percent. This industrial shift from manufacturing to services has had large environmental benefits for major cities from New York to Pittsburgh to Chicago. This trend is not unique to the United States. Over the last thirty years, London has lost 600,000 manufacturing jobs—and gained 600,000 jobs in business services, as well as 180,000 jobs in entertainment, leisure, hotels, and catering.[5] The transition from manufacturing to finance and services has increased the number of urbanites who have a financial stake in maintaining their city's high quality of life. Tourism and quality of life are key components helping modern, wealthy cities stay successful. Tourists want to see pretty things, like a nice ferry boat to the Statue of Liberty. All of this provides politicians with strong incentives to provide livable, green cities.

Up to this point, and in sharp contrast to crime and urban air and water pollution, climate conditions have been fixed. You can't make your city more sunny or less snowy. San Diego has nicer weather than Detroit. But all of that's about to change: a city whose climate amenities improve due to climate change (think of Fargo) will enjoy a windfall as more skilled people move to the area. The tax base will increase, financing improvements in local services such as public schools. If enough wealthy people move to the region, this local purchasing power will create a snowball effect, as fancier restaurants locate near such sophisticated consumers. A yuppie city will emerge thanks to the shift in the city's underlying climate amenities.

## Some Gutsy Predictions

To predict how climate change will affect city quality of life, climate modelers are actively building better and better models of how specific geographical areas' climates will change under different global greenhouse gas emissions growth scenarios. Whew. That mouthful means that climate modelers are using computers to predict local futures. The payoff of such computer crunching is a series of scenarios about future summer heat waves, sea level rise, and rainfall patterns.

In more than 3,100 U.S. counties, the Community Climate System Model (CCSM) computer model predicts that between now and the late twenty-first century, the typical county's average annual temperature will rise 8 degrees F, and its rainfall will decline by 0.3 inch. But these averages mask huge variations. The model predicts that there are 150 counties whose average temperature will rise by *only* 3 degrees F, and there are 150 counties whose average temperature will rise by *more than* 12 degrees F. Iowa and North Dakota are examples of states that are expected to grow much warmer. In the case of North Dakota, this is likely to make it a more attractive place to live. Historically, the average February temperature in North Dakota has been a frigid 15 degrees F. The CCSM model predicts that this will double to 30 degrees F by the end of this century, while August average temperatures will rise from 69 to 83 degrees F.

Some of the most dire computer predictions focus on the fate of coastal cities. Over the last sixty years more and more people have chosen to live in coastal U.S. cities from San Diego to Boston. Counties located within 50 miles of an ocean or a Great Lake coast make up just 13 percent of the continental

U.S. land area, but they accounted for 50 percent of the U.S. population in 2000 and 56 percent of the civilian income in 1999. Income per square kilometer in those counties is more than eight times that of inland counties.[6] The picture that emerges of these coastal cities is both densely populated and rich, because their amenities and climate attract households. The same general patterns exist in the European Union (EU). One-third of the EU population is estimated to live within fifty kilometers of the coast. The proportion is as high as 100 percent in Denmark and 75 percent in the United Kingdom and the Netherlands.[7] We have chosen to put ourselves at risk from rising sea levels. This coastal migration pattern has actually led us to suffer more from hurricanes and other storms because of the sheer quantity of people and property now built up along the coasts.

Although coastal cities are beautiful, if we really do fear what climate change has in store for us, many of us will move inland. If we are convinced that climate change will take place gradually, meaning that we will not wake up one morning and find that the sea level has risen two feet, then we can "wait and see." If climate change does raise the sea level, we will retreat from the coasts and invest in raising the structures that are close to the coast.

This strategy makes perfect sense—unless the disastrous scenario of abrupt climate change unfolds. In this case, a coastal city could disappear in the blink of an eye due to sudden sea level rise. If we actually believe that such nightmare tipping point scenarios have some chance of occurring, then we should seriously consider evacuating such cities. That said, I know of no current climate models making such dramatic predictions.

## Some Specifics from San Diego

Some rich cities are commissioning crystal ball studies to provide a glimpse of what they might look like in the medium term in a hotter world. In the case of San Diego, its study concluded that by 2050 its sea level will be 12 to 18 inches higher and the average annual temperature will increase 4.5 degrees F. The region will require 37 percent more water (relative to the period between 2001 and 2005), but the supply of water from sources such as the Colorado River will be smaller by 20 percent or more. Climate change will cause the fire season to start earlier, and the annual number of days with ideal conditions for big wildfires will increase by up to 20 percent. Peak electricity demand will increase by more than 70 percent.[8] Basic demographic trends predict that San Diego's senior citizen population will increase sharply at the same time that these changes are taking place. Seniors are typically less nimble in migrating in response to "new news" and are likely to be more sensitive to heat extremes and ambient pollution than younger people.

Although these predictions should be treated with caution, they do provide a useful heads-up for San Diego politicians. Consider the predictions of increased water shortages and soaring peak electricity demand. What underlies both of these predictions are two other predictions, of how many people are likely to be living in the San Diego area in 2050 and what their average income is likely to be. Richer people demand more power and water per capita, and the sheer size of the region scales up the demand. Hotter summers will translate into greater peak demand for air conditioning.

The weakness in a predictive analysis such as this one is predicting future technological advance. I do not see how the forecasters can know what the typical air conditioner's energy efficiency will be in the year 2050. If they are assuming that future air conditioners will be only as efficient as air conditioners in the year 2010, then they are likely to vastly overstate energy demand caused by the need for cooling on hot days. But even with this caveat, this exercise is useful for helping San Diego's leaders plan for necessary power generation and water conservation measures so that the city's inhabitants in the year 2050 can be confident that they will have access to these necessities in a hotter world.

Up and down the California coast, forecasters are predicting the extent of sea level rise. The Pacific Institute estimates that a 1.4-meter sea level rise will put 480,000 people at risk of experiencing a major flood event. These 480,000 people each face a 1 percent annual risk of being exposed to a major flood.[9] For those of you who slept through your intro statistics classes, this is similar to playing Russian roulette with a gun that has one bullet and one hundred chambers. But remember, people are not chained to their current homes. If the threat of a rising sea level is understood, then more people will choose to not live in the most at-risk flood zones. Those who remain can be encouraged to live in the floating homes that Brad Pitt is developing for New Orleans. Just because we face risk now does not mean that we have to face future risk. If we take these forecasts seriously, we will respond now and reduce our exposure—we'll adapt. Some California households may view the coastal areas as too risky and the inland areas as too hot. Households that had hoped to live on the California coast but now view it as too risky may choose to move inland to Idaho or Montana. The Pacific Institute predicts that in the San Francisco Bay Area, the population vulnerable to serious flooding is around 140,000 people (based on year 2000 data). An increase in sea level of 0.5 meter has only a modest effect on the number of people at risk. A 1.4-meter increase in sea level, however, doubles the number of people at risk from a one-hundred-year flood, to 270,000.[10] The price tag for protecting such vulnerable areas from flooding by building seawalls and levees will be at least $14 billion (in year 2000 dollars), with added maintenance costs of another $1.4 billion per year.

The extra risk caused by an additional 1.4 meters of sea water affects 130,000 people who currently do not face flood risk. In a metropolitan area of over 3 million people, 130,000 is a relatively small number. The people living in areas at risk from flooding can take precautions to protect themselves. Put simply, they can read the report and move out, and this inland migration would protect them. Adults can read the Pacific

Institute's report. If they continue to live in the flood zone, I am not convinced that they are "victims" just as I am not convinced that the hotel developers who put new construction in flood plains are "victims" of climate change when a shock hits. As we get ready for climate change, the public will have to admit that they are adults. Some may hope that the benevolent, paternalistic state will step in and protect us, but this borders on wishful thinking. In a nation of 300 million people, even the smart Obama administration would have trouble figuring out who is a victim and who is not. Anyone who took a gamble and regrets it after the fact, such as those who bet on the Colts in the 2010 Super Bowl, would appeal to the benevolent state for a bailout.

I recognize that the urban poor will need a nudge to protect themselves against the challenges that climate change will pose. If coastal areas become riskier because of climate change, and this lowers real estate prices there, the area will become a poverty magnet, attracting the poorest of the poor. Think of New Orleans' ninth ward and who is likely to live there as storm risk increases. Anticipating this challenge, environmental justice advocates would be wise to lobby for land zoning changes that rezone at-risk land as wetlands rather than as housing. Resettlement of urban minority communities raises a host of awkward issues. Past government efforts, such as the U.S. Housing and Urban Development's Move to Opportunity (MTO) program, have shown the benefits to poor households of moving to unfamiliar but higher-quality neighborhoods.[11] Teenage girls who move from ghetto areas to lower-poverty areas under this MTO program do better in school and are less likely to become involved in risky behaviors.[12]

In a diverse population, some people will be willing to gamble and continue to seek to live on the coast. One of my favorite teachers at the University of Chicago told us that a major idea in economics is that "deaf people should live next to airports." He had nothing against the hearing impaired and did not mean to offend them. His point was that given that you are deaf, the noise from airports disturbs you less than a person who can hear the noise. Because homes close to the airport are cheaper than homes that are farther away, deaf people actually enjoy a "free lunch" by living near the airport. They gain access to quality, cheap housing but do not suffer from the noise. In a similar sense, as climate change unfolds, coastal locations will still be beautiful, but it will be more risky to live there. Daredevils who recognize the risk but enjoy taking gambles will be attracted to these areas.

## How Will At-Risk Cities Compete in Our Hotter World?

It's important to consider the Watergate questions, What do people know, and when do they know it? If climate change's impact on your city primarily translates into increased heat waves, drought, and increased summer pollution (due to heat), then you will quickly feel it. But suppose climate change is a "silent killer," with no day-to-day symptoms—for example, in a port city whose risk of complete submersion increases dramatically. In this case, on a typical day the population may not perceive an objective change in the city's quality of life.

The city won't feel like a sinking ship. A sinking ship is a lost cause. When it reaches the bottom of the ocean, it will provide nice housing for some sea creatures and will give future divers the opportunity to have their own PBS documentary. A city at risk from climate change differs from a sinking ship in one key dimension of perception. Anyone can stare at a ship and decide that it's sinking, but a "sinking city" is in the eye of the beholder. If people believe that a city is not at risk from sea level rise, heat waves, and other climate change blows, then that city's landowners, politicians, and incumbent industries will benefit. Their kingdom will live on. In this sense, there is a financial incentive to cover up the fact that climate change creates objective risk for a certain subset of cities. These cities will have an incentive to hide this information.

Such conspiratorial cover-ups are a common theme in popular environmentalist culture's view of big business. Hollywood has generated many hit movies based on the cynical idea that selfish businesspeople make big profits while exposing the unsuspecting public to serious environmental risks (think of Mr. Burns on *The Simpsons*). The heroes in these movies are the whistle-blowers who won't let Mr. Big get away with it. Whether it is John Travolta playing a lawyer battling polluting factories in *A Civil Action* or Julia Roberts discovering a power plant's poisoning of a town's water supply in *Erin Brockovich*, the studio executives know that the public enjoys rooting for the righteous little guy in his fight against Goliath. These snapshots of popular culture reveal deep cynicism about capitalist growth and the motives of major capitalist firms. A clear picture is painted of firms run by greedy people who seek solely to make profits, regardless of the impacts on unsuspecting people or the natural environment.

The core issue here is "inside information." The firms know something that the public (the residents who live near the polluter and workers at the dirty factory) are unaware of. The public would make different choices if they knew the truth. Because nobody knows what the villain has done, he can't be held accountable. When watching movies, viewers have feelings of vengefulness and satisfaction when the villain's deeds are revealed in the end.

At-risk cities, such as Venice, have the same incentives as the corporate "Mr. Big," to suppress information about the city's health in the face of climate change. Climate disasters are low-probability, high-loss events. If no nasty flooding events have occurred in Venice for thirty years, then the mayor can declare that the city is safe. There is no evidence (except for climate model predictions) that this optimistic claim is false. Optimistic people will want to believe it. In the competition between cities, Venice can only be punished if households are wary about the risk they face living and visiting there, and if there are cities that are similar to Venice in terms of history and amenities but that face less climate risk. Given its features and history, Venice is a unique city, well aware that tourists will keep visiting their golden goose. A tourist-centered city at risk has no incentive to scare anyone away. This narrow pursuit of self-interest creates the possibility of tragedy if a low-probability flood does occur.

Although economics is called the dismal science, my field does offer some optimism about how to pry loose inside information about the true risks that cities face as they cope with climate change. Scholars who have studied competition between businesses in the same industry have noted that the competition gains when rumors about and smears of its rivals become public. When I was a kid, I loved a bubble gum called Bubble Yum that was produced by Life Savers. A rumor spread that there were spider eggs in the gum.[13] The company that made this product was forced to take out full-page advertisements in the *New York Times* to counter these claims. I have not crunched the data, but I bet that Bubble Yum's competitors gained at the Life Savers company's expense. This logic suggests that tourist destinations that compete with Venice will have strong incentives to contrast their charms and relative safety with Venice. It is unknown whether Venice politicians will simply dismiss these claims as lies by desperate opponents. The key here is whether tourists and the next generation of potential home buyers in Venice believe these claims. If they do and start to shy away from visiting, then city politicians will be pushed to take steps to convince people that Venice remains safe even in the face of climate change.

## Do Greens Do It Better?

The physical location of a city determines many of the direct challenges that climate change poses. A coastal city located below sea level faces greater threats from climate change than does Denver. But it would be a mistake to engage in geographical determinism. There are a number of strategies that a city can embrace to minimize the impact of climate change. Whether a city chooses this agenda hinges on who lives there. Contrast a city filled with Rush Limbaughs with another city filled with Al Gores.

In green cities such as Boston, San Francisco, Seattle, and Portland, young, highly educated, liberal people cluster, fostering an environmentalist spirit. Ambitious politicians such as the mayor of San Francisco, Gavin Newsom, actively campaign on a green policy agenda. In Portland successful political campaigning led to the transformation of Harbor Drive and helped to connect the city to the waterway.[14] The completion of the expensive Boston Big Dig has increased green space after removing the city's rusting 1960s highways.

Such liberal/environmentalist cities attract individuals who genuinely care about having a small footprint and want to live with others with similar tastes. Once such green paradises form, they feed on themselves. Take Berkeley, California. I live there several months a year, and it seems that every other registered vehicle is a Prius and solar panels virtuously hang on many roofs. The Berkeley community is walking the walk as its residents use public transit, drive less, and are more likely to be vegetarian than the average person. Such a city's residents are well versed in the basic climate research highlighting climate change's likely impacts. This extra knowledge makes them wise voters and consumers in the face of climate change.

Environmentalist cities also tend to be highly educated. People with more education are usually more patient and more likely to support costly investments that address long-term environmental threats.[15] More-educated people are more likely to demand in-depth analysis of environmental issues. This sets a virtuous cycle in motion by providing incentives for the media to research and present stories on pollution and the environment. People with more education play a more active political role. Such voters will actively seek out policies that simultaneously shrink the city's carbon footprint and protect it from likely climate change impacts.

A righteous city filled with Al Gore clones could pursue several adaptation strategies. It could update building codes and implement smart-growth principles to push developers to avoid building in flood and fire zones and build more climate-friendly, compact, and fire-resistant buildings. Such a city would figure out how to take advantage of shade and plant trees to minimize the urban heat island effect. This city would price electricity and water to encourage efficiency and conservation.[16] None of these policies is costless, but environmentalist cities will be more likely to make these sacrifices. The residents of such a city will eagerly sign up to buy the first-generation green cars, solar panels, and other energy-efficient products that help people both mitigate their carbon emissions and adapt to changing climate and economic conditions.

These cities offer other cities long-term benefits. Although Dick Cheney and friends enjoy making fun of nuclear-free zones such as Berkeley, if such progressive cities do choose to install solar panels and other first-generation technologies, this will create a nascent market demand. Such profit opportunities will attract firms to locate nearby that will develop expertise in installation and maintenance of such products. With experience, new discoveries will be made that will reduce the cost and raise the quality of these new technologies. Through this process, other cities around the United States will gain, because in the near future they will have the option of purchasing these green economy products that were perfected in the Berkeleys.

## Green Cities versus Climate-Safe Cities

Like anybody else, Al Gore wants to live in a city with a high quality of life that is safe from climate change. He has the money to be able to pay for such expensive real estate. Where would he want you to live? Suppose that Al Gore must assign households to live in either Boston or Houston. Suppose that Boston residents are at risk from climate change–related shocks, but that its residents have a very small carbon footprint—our hypothetical Boston residents use public transit, drive little, and consume electricity generated by renewable power plants that have low carbon emissions. In contrast, suppose that Houston is the opposite of Boston. Its residents face no direct risks from climate change, but households in Houston have a huge carbon footprint: they drive individual cars, eat meat, and use electricity generated by dirty, coal-fired power plants.

Al Gore has a tough choice: should he send people to Houston or Boston? There is no "win-win" here. People sent to Houston will be safe from scary climate change risks such as flooding, but the world's aggregate carbon emissions will increase, and this will exacerbate the impact of climate change for everyone else. People sent to Boston will be "human shields" and at risk, but the global externality of greenhouse gases will not be made worse. What should Al do? If his sole goal is climate change mitigation, he ships us to Boston. If he wants to protect us from climate change–induced harm, he sends us to Houston.

In a perfect world, our cities would offer Houston's protection and Boston's small footprint. In our real world, cities lie somewhere in between these extremes. If we all lived in "at-risk" Boston, we would be aware that we will suffer greatly from climate change. Out of narrow self-interest, we would vote for policies that protect us from climate change. In contrast, if we were "cocooned" in Houston, we would not feel this urgency and would view costly carbon mitigation regulation as a transfer; that is, we would face higher prices for fossil fuels, but other people (who live in climate risk cities) would gain from our financial sacrifice. A climate-safe city (Houston in this case) can actually hinder building an international coalition willing to sacrifice to mitigate carbon now. Al Gore and the Sierra Club will probably not admit it, but they need "human shields" to help them build a coalition of the willing who will vote for $4-per-gallon gas and the other costly steps we need to take to seriously reduce our global carbon emissions. If we do not expect to suffer at all from climate change, then only altruists will vote for significant regulation. There are not enough altruists in the United States to get Congress to sign such regulation.

## Naming the Low-Carbon Cities

No city actively competes to be named "the lowest-carbon city" in the United States. But the cities with a small per capita carbon footprint are being good global citizens. In a time when the United States produces more than 20 percent of the world's greenhouse gas emissions, these green cities are helping to mitigate the global challenge of reducing atmospheric carbon. So who is the greenest? In recent research, I ranked sixty-six of America's largest cities for their household carbon dioxide emissions.[17]

The rankings are highly intuitive. San Francisco scored a much higher green ranking than Houston. Relative to a green city such as San Francisco, Houston's humid summer climate requires much more electricity consumption for air conditioning. Houston's cheaper housing encourages households to buy more housing, which increases their energy consumption.

Houston's low population density and dispersed employment means that people rely on the private vehicle for transportation, and few use public transit. Houston's electricity is generated by dirtier power plants than San Francisco's electricity. A majority of California's power is produced by natural gas–fired power plants rather than dirtier coal-fired power plants. My study quantifies cross-city differences in the year 2000.[18] It is an open question how this ranking of cities would change in the presence of a carbon tax.

From the standpoint of reducing our nation's aggregate greenhouse gas production, government regulations should facilitate the construction of new housing in such low-carbon cities. But ironically, this is not the case. The cities with the smallest carbon footprint are the least likely to permit new housing to be built. On one level this is not surprising, because environmentalists choose to live in areas without sprawl, where open space is protected. A city such as San Francisco features a climate, population density, and a set of power plants (using natural gas rather than coal) that add up to a low-carbon footprint. But new housing permitting is determined at the local level, and for better or worse, liberal/green cities engage in a form of NIMBYism (not in my back yard) that deflects growth to other cities that are more pro-growth.

## Naming the Most Climate-Resilient Cities

When I was a kid I loved to the read the *Book of Lists*. Although I do not remember the list of famous people who died during sexual intercourse, I do have a vague memory of the worst places to hitchhike, people misquoted by Ronald Reagan, and breeds of dogs that bite people the most. Now that I am old enough to write books, I feel the urge to contribute my own list, of cities both in the United States and around the world that have the best chance to be safe as climate change unfolds.

In forming this list, I would like to be scientific about my methods. It is quite difficult to compare cities with respect to the set of adaptation policies they now have and will have in the medium future. I recognize that such policies (such as zoning to push housing away from flood zones) will help cities to adapt to climate change blows, but I focus on characteristics of cities that we know will persist over time and will help them to cope with climate change.

With this caveat, here is my list of the top five climate resilient U.S. cities:

1.  Salt Lake City
2.  Milwaukee
3.  Buffalo
4.  Minneapolis
5.  Detroit

It is no accident that these cities are away from the coasts. Although climate change will throw a variety of punches, sea level rise is the nastiest challenge of them all. Elevated, inland Salt Lake City and the other cities on the list will not flood.[19] It is also no accident that the cities on this list all are located in northern parts of the United States. Their summers are not so hot right now, and unlike Phoenix, they will not bake in summer time. As far as I know, none of these cities faces issues of drought or ambient air pollution.[20]

Who would want to live in these cities? Scaredy cats who want some certainty in their lives will value the safety offered by such cities in our hotter world. Young people know that they can wait and see, then migrate if their city deteriorates, but the elderly are much less likely to move. The developed world is getting older. In England today there are more than 10,000 people over the age of 100 and more than 400 people over the age of 105.[21] As the average age of the population rises, some people will prefer to move to a safe city while they are young and remain there.

The extremely risk averse will be the most likely to seek out these cities in a hotter world; the rest of us face tradeoffs. Cities such as San Francisco will continue to have many attractive features. In a riskier future, the safest cities will have a better chance to compete with the best cities in the United States. I recognize that I am taking geography very seriously, but at the end of the day the location of cities is a key distinguishing feature of different cities with hundreds of thousands or millions of people each. Although I have not tried to incorporate adaptation policy choices into my rankings, it should be clear that a city such as Salt Lake City, which faces relatively little climate change risk, can get away with engaging in fewer adaptive policies than can a more at-risk city such as New York or Los Angeles.

Turning to the rest of the world, I am willing to name names. Moscow scores high on my list, as do Berlin, Paris, Krakow, Calgary, and Beijing. These cities are away from the coast and unlikely to suffer significant flood damage. Each is located to the north and is unlikely to become unbearably hot compared to other cities in the same nation. Warmer winters are always a highly valued amenity, and each of these cities will benefit from climate change–induced winter warmth.

You must have noted the absence of major U.S. superstar cities on my domestic list of resilient cities. As a landowner in one of those cities (Los Angeles) and the son of landowners in another of those cities (New York), this concerns me. Chapters 4 and 5 discuss how these superstar cities will cope in our hotter world. By drilling down into specific cities, I can narrow the geographical focus and examine not only how climate change affects cross-city competition (the theme of this chapter) but also how different communities in the same major cities are affected.

# 4

# PLAYING ONE-ON-ONE WITH KOBE BRYANT

**L**os Angeles is a hedonist's paradise. At night, you can cruise the Sunset Strip. Although The Doors no longer play there, you may run into Paris Hilton or Britney Spears before seeing Brad Pitt and Angelina Jolie at a red-carpet event. During the winter, you might venture downtown to watch Kobe Bryant and the Lakers play. Every day of the year you can sit outside at Starbucks and try to identify professional basketball players looking for a latte in West Los Angeles. In spring 2009 I spotted Baron Davis of the Los Angeles Clippers at a Westwood Starbucks (but he didn't seem to recognize me). In fall 2009 I spotted Brian Wilson of the Beach Boys as he strolled in Little Holmby Park (he didn't give me a knowing nod or wink either). I saw Vin Diesel jog past my house not long ago (again, no seeming recognition on his part). Even the dignified former secretary of state, Warren Christopher, didn't recognize me as he got out of his car while parking on my block. These cases suggest that I'm not a VIP, but a player such as you will have the option of ending the night at a party at the Playboy Mansion near UCLA.

During the day, LA also offers a variety of natural pleasures. The outdoors is an essential part of every Los Angeles resident's day-to-day life. Almost every day you can jog along the Santa Monica and Venice paths near the Pacific Ocean. In the afternoon you can go for a mountain climb in Topanga Park in the Santa Monica Mountains. You can walk around in shorts in February, and in the summer there is rarely humidity or a heat wave. If you are depressed, the blue skies and the ocean breeze will cheer you up. Graduate students at UCLA drive me nuts because they surf in February rather than studying or grading exams. The city feels like an unending adult summer camp. Flowers bloom in late February, and you can e-mail your friends in the Northeast and mock them by singing Pink Floyd's "Wish You Were Here." Although everyone is always talking on hands-free cell phones, nobody here actually works for "the man"; LA is not a company town. The largest corporate employers in Los Angeles County are Kaiser Permanente, with 32,000 employees; Northrop Grumman Corp., with 21,000 employees; and Boeing Co., with 15,000 employees. Of course Los Angeles is famous for Hollywood. The motion picture and television show production sector is responsible for roughly 250,000 jobs.[1] In a county with 8 million people, this shows that most people are small wheeler dealers.

Almost everyone in Los Angeles was not born here. Many of us are transplants from cold Northeastern cities. Although we differ in heritage and ethnicity, we share a love for the sun and the good life. This city self-selects people who want to live well. With the exception of me, we are well-tanned, physically fit, attractive people. There is an abundance of plastic surgeons; service providers offering you whiter teeth; swimming pools; and life coaches to pluck, wax, and generally improve every part of your body and mind.

Outsiders mock Los Angeles as a city of plagues. They have heard about the car culture, the sprawl, traffic, the smog, O.J., the gangs, the earthquakes, the Malibu fires, the water shortages, and so on. But to residents of Los Angeles, traffic is the only constant menace. Los Angelenos' average one-way commute time of twenty-nine minutes is a result of many people working at home (their zero-commute time balances out the long commutes).[2] On the roads there are many fancy cars both because people can afford them and because people spend so much time stuck in traffic.

To a New Yorker (I lived in Manhattan for thirteen years and in the New York metro area for twenty-five), Los Angeles really is a strange city. Whereas most cities have a downtown featuring a vibrant employment and cultural center, Los Angeles's downtown is not such a magnet. Yes, the Lakers play there, the University of Southern California is there, and Frank Gehry has built a funky Walt Disney Concert Hall there, but these three provide insufficient gravitational force to encourage the rest of Los Angeles to go downtown. My UCLA students tell me that they never go downtown and have no desire to.

I am a recent LA home buyer. I made the brilliant financial move of purchasing in May 2008. When we bought our house, we made an implicit bet that Los Angeles would remain a great place to live and work. I have my fingers crossed. Home prices in Los Angeles are more than double those in other major cities. In 2008 the average single-family home in Los Angeles County sold for $578,000, and 10 percent of the homes in the county sold for more than $1,000,000. There are more than 32,000 zip codes in the United States. Of the top 200 zip codes ranked by average housing price in the entire United States, 45 percent are in California, although only 20 percent of the nation's population lives in California. Twenty of the top 200 most expensive U.S. zip codes are in Los Angeles County, including Beverly Hills 90210.

These high prices are not due to the inherent productivity of working in Los Angeles. In fact, my time spent outside in the sun while in Los Angeles has probably made me a worse economist. Economists at the University of Chicago claim that Chicago's bad weather raises their productivity by eliminating the option of playing tennis. Los Angeles's great quality of life is what drives up local home prices. The average buyer of a single-family house in Los Angeles County in 2008 paid $324 per square foot of interior space. If LA's quality of life declines, my life savings will unravel.

Climate change can't alter the blue skies or access to the beach and mountains, but it will pose four tangible threats: The summers will grow hotter, the air will be smoggier, there will be more fires, and there will be much less water. In other words, as we saw in chapter 3, climate change is going to shift the competitive landscape of cities, and LA is going to take a hit. And the poorest parts of LA are going to be hurt worst of all. But there's a lot we can learn from an examination of LA's probable future—especially the basic lesson that prices matter. Other cities take note. Our tour of LA will show us the key role that market prices of both electricity and water will play in determining this city's fate. In addition, this case study will highlight how government policy (such as binding land use zoning and caps on water prices) can unintentionally hinder adaptation.

### Will LA Lose Its Cool?

California's cool summers and warm winters distinguish its cities from the rest of the nation. Southern cities are hot and humid in summer. Midwestern and Eastern cities are cold in the winter and humid in the summer. Nobody wants to be in Houston or Washington, D.C., in the middle of summer. In contrast, in Los Angeles today the average temperature in July is 74 degrees F, with little humidity.

Climate change will likely degrade LA's ideal climate. Leading climate researchers have developed two different models that allow them to predict each U.S. county's average temperature and rainfall by month for the years 2070 to 2099. Two computer models, with the catchy names CCSM Model and H3A1FI Model, bear bad news. Los Angeles County is predicted to be 13 degrees F warmer on average in July by 2070. The problem for current LA real estate owners (such as myself) is that a fair bit of the value of their assets (my home) rests on the fact that relatively few areas in the United States feature warm winters and cool summers. In the future LA's climate will look like Jacksonville, Florida's, climate today. This is bad news for my housing wealth.

You might try to soothe my spirits by reminding me that all cities will face hotter summers. Unfortunately for you, dear reader, I know the lost art of statistics. I have crunched the data to study the relationship between county home prices and county climate conditions. What jumps out from this analysis is that areas with cool summers and warm winters command a huge real estate price premium. There are relatively few such areas (mostly in California), and they are in high demand. Climate change is predicted to strip away much of California's climate uniqueness, and therefore will strip away the housing price boost that comes with that climate. Mean July temperatures close to 90 degrees F by the late twenty-first century will force down relative real estate prices to reflect underlying changes in climate amenities.

Climate change will cause the most "amenity havoc" for cities in California. San Francisco, San Diego, and Los Angeles are all expected to be big climate amenity losers. The one piece of good news is that California's major cities are not expected to become much more humid. Climate experts do not believe that there are any plausible scenarios in which California becomes much more humid in summertime in general. After all, climate change is not going to change the fundamentally dry subtropical climate of this region in summer.

In contrast, cities in Florida will actually experience an improvement in their climate bundle as winter temperatures increase (an amenity) and summer average temperatures rise relatively little. Only three major U.S. metropolitan areas are expected to experience an improvement in their climate bundle due to climate change. These are Las Vegas, Fort Lauderdale, and West Palm Beach. In the case of Las Vegas, its climate bundle will improve because of predicted increases in rainfall.

A critic of these climate prediction models would be appalled that they predict an average temperature over an enormous land area such as Los Angeles County, which is more than 4,000 square miles. By definition, such an "average" prediction must mask huge variations. In areas of West Los Angeles such as Santa Monica and Malibu, the cool breeze off the Pacific Ocean will cool the expensive homes of the elite. But inland, in East Los Angeles and the San Fernando Valley, temperatures already soar into the 100s in summer and are likely to be much hotter in the face of climate change. This suggests that small pockets of West Los Angeles, such as expensive Santa Monica, Brentwood, and Westwood, could actually grow more valuable as the rest of Los Angeles becomes less inhabitable. Millions of people who live in expensive San Fernando Valley homes will suffer from home price declines as their climate amenity premium vanishes.

The poor and immigrants will bear the brunt of exposure to heat waves and midsummer extreme temperatures. As a point of comparison, consider the Chicago heat wave of 1995, which disproportionately killed members of elderly poor black households in the center city. They did not own air conditioners, and their fear of crime led them to not open their windows. The public health consequences of such heat waves depend on whether "victims" know that a heat wave is coming and have access to coping strategies. Not everyone can jump on a plane and head to Idaho for a week during the peak heat.

We count on public service announcements to alert people of an impending event, such as a smog alert (when ambient air pollution is expected to be above a critical threshold level that threatens public health) or a heat wave, or in Asia that a tsunami is brewing. But how do we inform groups that face language and cultural barriers? In inland Los Angeles, the population is mostly Hispanic. Many of the members of these households do not speak fluent English, and some are in the United States illegally. Such individuals are unlikely to be interested in or willing to follow information provided by government sources. These are exactly the people who are most at risk from the shock. Fortunately, community-based NGOs have stepped up to fill this void. In Eastern Los Angeles, one example is the Esperanza's Community Health Programs, which has been involved in the community by providing access to health information. Such unheralded "little guys" help a diverse city prepare for heat wave challenges.

## The Return of Smog?

Given its topography and climate patterns and the scale of economic activity in the metropolitan area, the Los Angeles Basin suffers from some of the highest levels of air pollution in the United States. During the 1970s, before the introduction of stringent new vehicle emissions regulation that began in California in 1972, LA was the smog capital. Millions of people were driving high-emitting vehicles. Polluting oil-refining activity in the Long Beach area contributed to the local smog problem. Old, dirty diesel trucks carrying goods from the Port of Long Beach to consumers around the United States helped to scale up deadly particulate matter concentrations.

In the 1970s and early 1980s, smog levels were awful in Los Angeles. Starting in the mid-1990s, ambient ozone declined sharply in Los Angeles County. Across eight monitoring stations that monitored ambient ozone in 1980 and in 2000, the average annual pollution daily excedence (when air pollution exceeds the Clean Air Act standard) count for these eight monitors declined from 103 days per year to 13 days per year.

These pollution gains are especially notable because between 1980 and 2000, the Los Angeles Basin's population grew by 42 percent and total automobile mileage grew by 88 percent. Vehicle emissions control regulation deserves a lot of credit. New cars today are 95 percent cleaner than new cars built in the early 1970s. These emissions control improvements persist over time even as the vehicle ages. Put simply, emissions per mile of driving have decreased faster over time in Los Angeles than miles driven have increased.

Climate change could reverse some of this progress. The details of atmospheric chemistry concerning how volatile organic compounds and oxides of nitrogen mix to form ozone are complicated, but it can be said that heat waves are likely to cook up more summertime smog. Smog problems will grow the most away from the ocean, in East Los Angeles. Relative to West Los Angeles, East LA's communities are poorer and have more Hispanic residents. Due to this differential pollution exposure across demographic groups, climate change will bring environmental justice concerns to the forefront.

It is no surprise that wealthy, white households live in cool, clean West Los Angeles, while poorer Hispanics are more likely to live in the hot, smoggy eastern section of the city. For homes that sold in 2008, the average price of a home declined by 1.4 percent with each kilometer of distance from the beach. This housing price gradient guarantees that wealthy people will cluster closer to the high-amenity area.

If climate change increases smog exposure for poor minorities, this would reverse twenty years of progress in achieving environmental justice goals due to effective Clean

Air Act regulation. In earlier work, I documented that between 1980 and 2000, the average Hispanic household in Los Angeles was exposed to thirty fewer smoggy days a year because of disproportionate improvements in air quality in communities where Hispanics tend to live. Climate change may reverse this progress.

In Malibu, Barbra Streisand had access to clean air even in the early 1970s when the rest of the metropolitan area was terribly polluted. The Clean Air Act's success at reducing smog over the last thirty years has had little effect on Malibu and other coastal communities. Instead, it helped to bring about convergence between inland areas and the cool, clean coast. Clean Air Act regulation has narrowed this air pollution exposure gap between the haves and the have-nots.

This is another of the main lessons that LA can teach us: climate change is likely to affect the poor far worse than it does the rich. If Malibu did become unlivable for a few weeks a year, perhaps due to high heat or smoke from nearby fires, then Streisand and friends could retreat to a bucolic Montana cabin.

## The Death of Green Grass?

When I lived in New York City, I had never heard of koi ponds. Having lived in Westwood for three years, I am now an expert on them. They abound in Los Angeles. Although it rains only 11 inches per year in Los Angeles, millions of its residents expect to be able to shower, flush their toilets, water their beautiful lawn's grass, play golf on green fairways, and swim in Olympic-sized private pools. As incomes in this mega-city have grown, people have come up with new ways to consume water, including garden waterfalls that help block street noise.

Despite the fact that it rarely rains in Los Angeles, households in this desert area have no incentive to view water as a scarce commodity. They are charged less than one cent per gallon of water. Public water authorities refuse to engage in "price gouging," which makes voters happy in the short run—we get to enjoy our swimming pools and ample green grass. But it means that a day of reckoning lurks in the not-so-distant future. Low prices remove any incentive to get "lean and mean" and reduce one's water use. This low pricing creates a culture of waste. When my family goes for a walk in our neighborhood near UCLA, we are amazed at the gallons of water being used for watering the lawns and, due to broken pipes and other mishaps, just flooding the roads. Los Angeles has created a "hot line" for reporting such water wastage. Like an Eastern European living under communism, I have reported my neighbors to this "Secret Water Police."[3] Why? Although I dislike my neighbors, I especially dislike their wasting a scarce resource for no good reason. But nobody from City Hall has ever gotten in touch with me, and nobody has given me a medal.

One of the first lessons taught in an introductory economics course is that prices signal scarcity. Climate scientists are emphasizing that climate change will make water a much scarcer resource in the American West.[4] In California, there is great concern about climate change causing the melting of the Sierra Mountains snowpack. This will reduce the state's water supply. When a precious commodity becomes scarcer, the price should go up. When prices are allowed to fluctuate and reflect free-market supply and demand conditions, a low price means that a given commodity is plentiful. The irony is that California is already in drought, but prices are still very low. The reasons for cheap water pricing remain a mystery to me. (But I must confess that I also support European-style gas taxes; raise them to $2 per gallon, I say.)

A nonprofit called the Metropolitan Water District of Southern California sells the water to LA households.[5] The agency is not interested in maximizing its profits, nor does it seem very concerned right now about preparing for climate change. Needless to say, the agency disagrees with my pricing strategies.

Let's contrast the market for water with the market for high-quality coffee. Imagine if the mayor of Los Angeles seized control of all Starbucks located in his kingdom and ordered them to sell their products at a nickel per cup of coffee. Consumers would be happy for about a day as they received deep discounts on their triple lattes. But when the Starbucks shut down because the branches were losing money, the consumers would wish that the mayor would privatize this sector again and let prices rise. Because the Metropolitan Water District does not prioritize earning "profit" (revenue minus costs), the artificially low water prices can persist for a long time.[6]

These low prices lull California water consumers into a false sense that the water will continue to flow.

That attitude affects all (or nearly all; I'm exempt, but I'm an economist) Los Angelenos. Consider the case of Tony Villaragosa. Mr. Villaragosa is a successful UCLA graduate and is the mayor of Los Angeles. He is actively pursuing policies to make Los Angeles a "green city."[7] Yet this mayor used 386,716 gallons of water at his Mount Washington home in the year before he moved into the mayor's mansion in October 2005.[8] His water consumption was roughly double that of other households with similar-sized lots who live in his area. I would not call the mayor a hypocrite; I would say that he has responded to low water prices by not conserving. He is not alone. Of the 45,000 single-family homes in Los Angeles County that sold in 2008, 16 percent had swimming pools. In the subset of these homes that sold for more than $1 million, 35 percent had pools, and 46 percent of homes that sold for more than $5 million had pools. Presumably the founding fathers did not view private swimming pools as an inalienable right.

## How Do We Allocate Scarce Water?

Growing Southern California faces a fundamental water challenge. If we are serious about getting ready to adapt to climate change, then we must allow the prices of water and electricity to reflect their true scarcity. By reducing the supply of available water, climate change will create an imperative, forcing reluctant governments to recognize that water prices must reflect the basic fundamentals of supply and demand. If demand is rising (due to income and population growth) and supply is declining (due to climate change), then the water authorities face a choice between allowing prices to rise or setting up a complex rationing scheme. Rationing makes economists nuts because it is the equivalent of handing a vegetarian a meat pizza to eat and telling the vegetarian that he or she cannot trade it to a meat lover. The authorities are struggling to cope with these expected imbalances in supply and demand caused by ongoing economic growth and climate change.

The irony here is that you can pick up the *Los Angeles Times* once a week and see an article bemoaning California's "water shortage." In response to this "crisis," cities within the Los Angeles metro area such as the city of Long Beach have adopted serious water rationing policies, including limiting lawn watering to Monday, Thursday, and Saturday and placing time limits on the hours and timing when watering can take place. Any watering must be done between 6 P.M. and 7 A.M. and cannot last longer than ten minutes. People cannot wash down driveways, sidewalks, parking areas, patios, or other outdoor areas with water from a hose. Restaurants can only serve water upon request. Overwatering lawns to the point that there is runoff is illegal.[9]

Starting June 1, 2009, the Los Angeles Department of Water and Power has proudly announced that it is using prices to address the water shortage. To protect lower-income consumers, the first tier's prices remain unchanged, but the second pricing tier will increase by a whopping 44 percent.[10] The message is clear: the DWP is doing something. But it's not as impressive as it sounds.

In the case of water pricing in Los Angeles, something strange is hidden within the rate structure. People who live on larger properties pay less per gallon of water. Permit me to give you an example that strikes close to home. I live in the 90024 zip code. My home is within a half mile of Candy Spelling's $150-million mansion. She is the widow of Aaron Spelling (the father of *Charlie's Angels* and of Tori Spelling) and is seeking to sell her home.

Let's compare our respective water pricing schedules. According to the DWP pricing schedules, to remain on the first tier (the low pricing of water), you must know the square footage of your lot size and how many people live in your house. During the dry months of June to Halloween, homes whose lots are 7,500 square feet or smaller face a first-tier limit during the winter and spring of $28 \times 748$ gallons (every two months), whereas those who live on properties with a lot size of 43,560 square feet and larger (like Candy Spelling) stay on the first tier until they consume $76 \times 748$ gallons.[11]

A gallon of water is a gallon of water, and we should each pay the same price for using it. The state knows that it is in the middle of long-term drought. Leading researchers see a similarity between water conditions today and events during the twelfth century, when a particularly severe drought in Southern California was coupled with persistent low flows in the Sacramento and Colorado rivers, a situation that lasted about sixty years.[12]

Los Angeles has set up a system whereby rich people who own more grass actually pay a lower price per gallon of water consumed. In my "real world," when Candy Spelling and I each show up at the Westwood Starbucks, we each get charged the same price for an espresso. Facing this price, we make a "take it or leave it" decision. Unlike this "fair" pricing, she pays a lower average price per gallon of water than I do, because she has a bigger house! She is getting a better deal than me because she owns more grass! Implicitly, I am paying for a lot of watering of her grass. I present this case study not merely to earn your sympathy. My goal is to call out government for the unintended consequences of its policies. Climate change adaptation will be more difficult in Los Angeles because of its current policies.

Many environmentalists assume that big business is the cause of our environmental problems and that wise regulating government is the only honorable agent that can force these bad guys to act in the public's interest. But in this case it is government policies that are causing the adaptation challenge.

Economists love to talk about the consequences of bad incentives, but this borders on funny. There is serious drought in the West. Higher prices for water could encourage demand-side conservation. The Los Angeles Department of Water & Power is not doing its part to "solve" the problem. If the LADWP treated everyone equally and charged everyone the same price per gallon of water, or at least exposed everyone to the same tiered pricing schedule, this agency would either collect a lot more revenue from water sales to the rich with large lots, or owners of private "golf courses" (those with big swimming pools and lots of grass) would cut back on their water consumption.

Although they are wimping out on explicitly raising water prices to reflect "true scarcity," the California water providers are trying alternative incentive approaches for reducing water consumption. California households are offered a variety of rebates for "green" appliances, including

- ☼ high-efficiency clothes washers;
- ☼ high-efficiency toilets;
- ☼ weather-based irrigation controllers, or "smart" controllers;
- ☼ rotating sprinkler nozzles; and
- ☼ synthetic turf (limit one-half acre).[13]

These rebates encourage replacement of old, inefficient durables with these water-conserving devices, but this well-meaning "green" subsidy may actually increase water consumption when people continue to face a low price per gallon of water. People may now do more wash (and hence use more water) because the price per wash has declined. To illustrate this point, consider a car that needs one gallon of gas to drive 1 mile. If the price of gasoline is $3 a gallon, then owners of this gas guzzler will pay $3 to travel 1 mile. If the household is given a vehicle that can travel 30 miles per gallon, the price per mile falls to 10 cents per mile. If this household responds to this large drop in the price per mile by driving much more, then its total gasoline consumption could *increase* because it purchased a more fuel-efficient vehicle! Although I doubt that this "boomerang" effect is large, this example highlights the consequences of pursuing indirect means of reducing household resource consumption rather than simply using prices.

The water utilities are trying to incentivize people to economize on water and electricity consumption, but they are tying one hand behind their backs by taking the best policy option (higher prices) off the table. My mother-in-law got a chuckle recently when she received a check from her California water provider. This money was a reward for "saving water." According to her water bill, she had sharply reduced her water consumption relative to her baseline consumption. The water provider concluded this by comparing her recent water consumption with her previous water consumption (perhaps the previous year) over the same time period. What the water authority did not know was that she was in Italy for the entire billing cycle. She had not changed her day-to-day behavior; because she was out of the country, she was not using PGE water to flush the toilets, water the yard, or take a bath. But the water authority is not Big Brother. It does not know why her water consumption decreased (as determined by her Berkeley water meter falling to zero). Without knowing the true cause of her "conservation," PGE sent her a check that she would say she doesn't deserve.

## Engineering Solutions to Water Shortage?

Rising water prices would trigger innovation that could take some odd turns. There are new water technologies that can effectively increase the supply of water. Today, water desalinization is quite expensive. Somehow water recycling has been tarred with the name "toilet to the tap"—which is actually an accurate description of the idea.[14] Certainly anyone who doesn't trust engineering techniques would wonder whether the water is contaminated with fecal matter, but those who do trust the technology would be happy to guzzle it. Despite the science behind water recycling, in the late 1990s the Los Angeles mayor scuttled a plan that would have used this technology and mitigated water "shortages" in the city, because he was worried about voter backlash from the gross-out factor.

Today engineers continue to try to push support for projects such as the reuse of "gray water." Light gray water is wastewater from the shower, bath, bathroom sink, and clothes washer. Heavy gray water is wastewater from the kitchen sink and dishwasher. Commercial technologies already exist for processing both light and heavy gray water on-site for nonpotable usage.[15] Although the water produced is not clean enough to drink, such technologies effectively increase our supply of water for other basic uses. This is quite valuable in a world where water will become scarcer.

Engineering solutions to the challenges that Mother Nature poses are not always embraced. Consider putting fluoride in the water supply. This has helped to sharply reduce cavities and other tooth decay problems.[16] Recently economic research has documented that people with more teeth earn higher wages.[17] Differential access to fluoridated water during childhood offers a "natural experiment" for testing how this public health intervention affects long-term quality of life. One research team used adult wages as their key outcome measure and found that women who resided in communities with fluoridated water during childhood earn about 4 percent more than women who did not live in communities with fluoridated water.

Although this may not seem surprising to you, such research is necessary to help make the case that public health strategies such as putting fluoride in water improve our health and well-being. But controversy has arisen over this strategy. Some potentially valid concerns have arisen, such as that fluoride intake is not easily controlled and that children could be overdosed.[18] Other objections make less sense. In the 1950s, it was argued that water fluoridation was part of a communist plot.

Climate change will force Californians to have a serious policy discussion about water priorities. As water supplies decline, and if people reject engineering solutions such as the "toilet to the tap," what is to be done?

### Will California's Farmers Bail Out the City Slickers?

California farmers offer one possible source of supply. It is well known that 80 percent of the state's water goes to agriculture and that 40 percent of the state's water goes to growing four crops: cotton, rice, alfalfa, and pasturage (irrigated grazing land). These four crops account for only 1 percent of the state's annual income.[19] Urbanites generate California's wealth, but historical property rights allocations have granted the increasingly scarce water to farming interests.

An economics 101 student would say, "Let me get this right. Farmers have the property rights to this water and are growing low-profit crops such as alfalfa and strawberries while thirsty urbanites are willing to pay more than ten times as much for this same water that the farmers are using? Let the farmers sell their water to the urbanites and then California's cities will suffer less from climate change."

Unfortunately, many remember the "Theft of Owens Valley." Although these events took place in the 1920s, farmers have long memories. If water sellers today believe that past farmers did not receive a good deal from the first great water transfers, this will discourage trade today in water transfers.

The Owens Valley case continues to generate wide academic and popular attention. Consider the movie *Chinatown*. This Oscar-winning film helped Jack Nicholson pay for his Lakers front-row court seat and to perpetuate the myth that corrupt LA stole its life-sustaining water supply from unsuspecting Owens Valley farmers. Although leading economic historians have reevaluated and rejected this version of what happened, the "fact" remains that in the past city slickers outfoxed the rural farmers in a lopsided trade that led to the urbanites' being enriched at the rural area's expense.[20] To quote The Who, "We won't be fooled again."

Today's farmers are worried that history will repeat itself as they are suckered by the "big city" sophisticates into a deal that takes their water at too low a price. Climate change will make California's urbanites more desperate to find sources of water, and the farmers will have property rights to California's scarce water. A farmer who seeks to maximize profits would diversify his or her portfolio of assets and substitute growing less water-intensive crops and selling surplus water to the thirsty urbanites at a high price. Such privately beneficial actions by the farmer will help Southern California's cities adapt to climate change.

## Come on Baby, Light My Fire

When the Santa Ana winds pick up, you know it. These are surprisingly hot winds, with gusts of 40 miles per hour or higher. The streets of Los Angeles smell like a Boy Scout fire. The odor one smells is not S'mores cooking but rather Malibu homes ablaze. These fancy homes are located in fire zones. The rest of the country fixates on great television videos of multi-million-dollar Malibu celebrity homes burning down. Local media reports have reported that actors Matthew McConaughey and Minnie Driver were among those forced to evacuate in a recent fire, and Red Hot Chili Peppers bass guitarist Flea's home was destroyed by the flames. A text message from the rock star said his US$10.5-million mansion had "burnt to a crisp."

Today, climate modelers are uncertain whether climate change will increase fire risk. On the one hand, Los Angeles is predicted to receive 50 percent less rain than it does now, and the combination of less rain and more summer heat means a drier landscape that is more prone to fires. On the other hand, the frequency of Santa Ana winds is predicted to decline as the eastern deserts warm. Within Los Angeles, there is significant variation in the exposure to fire risk. People in the center city of Los Angeles or even Westwood face little risk from these fires, but in other areas such as Malibu, there could be significant fire risk posed by climate change.

There are several possible coping strategies to protect the city against future fire risk caused by climate change. The simplest would be to reduce new housing construction in fire zone regions by requiring homeowners there to pay significantly more for fire insurance. Alternatively, these households could be offered lower insurance premiums if they build their homes with fire-resistant materials and landscape their property so that their homes are less prone to fire risk. Although I hope that local political leaders would support such "safety first" policies, I am pessimistic that these policies could be adopted. Landowners would complain that these proposals represent a property "taking," stripping them of their development rights and exposing them to the whims of price-gouging insurance companies. They would argue that their 3,000-square-foot houses should have the same home insurance premiums as similar homes built elsewhere in Los Angeles. They would say that they are being discriminated against.

On some level, they are right. Different parcels of land face different risks from climate change's new blows. Those who own land in areas that we now know are risky (due to climate change) are losers. I am not convinced that society owes them compensation for losing a bet. Similar to the developers of the St. Louis hotels located in a flood plain, these fire zone landowners want to flip a one-sided coin. They want access to cheap insurance that bails them out if a nasty fire occurs, but they also want the right to live there as if the area is not at elevated risk because of climate change. If we are serious about tackling climate change, we need to design credible incentives to push more economic activity (and multi-million-dollar homes) away from geographical areas that are increasingly at risk because of climate change.

Consider fire protection in California communities at the wildland/urban interface. The biggest danger is where suburban communities abut forest lands, in counties such as Marin, Alameda, Contra Costa, and Santa Clara. In areas such as the Sierra Nevada foothills and the interior areas in Southern California, the scenery is beautiful but at greater risk from fire as climate change raises temperatures and reduces rainfall. When forest fires occur, a large amount of damage to life and property can quickly take place. California budgets $519 million for fighting wildfires, with an emergency $182-million fund. The state fights the fires with prison inmates; 4,400 are trained each year to do the grunt work. Given California's current large fiscal deficit, the governor has been planning to release prisoners earlier. An unintended consequence of this money-saving plan is a smaller firefighting force.

To my surprise, my California tax dollars are being used to pay for firefighting in this high-risk area. I naively assumed that people who live in these fire zones pay for their own extra fire protection services through local property taxes. But this is not the case. Climate change will increase both the size of these zones and the severity of risk that local residents face in them. Current state policy spreads the cost of this fire protection across all residents in the state. But consider a small change in state fire policy. If local governments in fire zones had to pay for the bulk of their own fire protection, they would change their zoning codes to allow less new development in these areas. This would immediately reduce the cost of climate change–induced forest fires.

### Los Angeles Has a Subway?

Public transit is not used in Los Angeles. In the year 2000, only 6 percent of LA residents commuted using public transit. The Santa Monica Big Blue bus charges adults 75 cents and students 25 cents a ride, yet this isn't enough of an incentive to lure mass ridership.

Although the car is cool, a more fundamental reason why people in Los Angeles do not walk, take the bus, or use the subway is that the city is so spread out. Urban researchers have documented that this city has at least sixteen different major employment centers, each with more than 100,000 jobs centered in it. Unlike nineteenth- and early twentieth-century cities, which had a single downtown employment center, the modern city has multiple employment centers. When people work in the suburbs, they are highly likely to commute by private vehicle.

The paradox is that the average Los Angeles resident lives in a neighborhood with 13,100 people per square mile, but few live a "new urbanist" lifestyle of walking and biking to places of work, shopping, and cultural activities. In recent years, the city and federal governments have invested billions of dollars in a subway and light rail system geared to getting people downtown. The Red Line is LA's subway. It was opened in early 1993, with extensions through Hollywood opened later in the 1990s. The total cost of building this system has been roughly $6 billion, or $300 million per mile. Today, 150,000 people per day ride this subway.[21] In contrast, 5 million per day ride the New York City subway.[22]

Today, Los Angeles is considering building a "Subway to the Sea." This east/west subway could take people from Hollywood, west through Beverly Hills, Westwood, Brentwood, and then finally to Santa Monica and the beach. My UCLA students tell me that they will take this subway (which will cost roughly $1 billion per mile) the 5 miles to the beach once it opens. If this subway does cost $5 billion to build, and if it attracts 200,000 riders per year, then after twenty-five years it will have attracted 5 million riders. The average fixed cost of providing this service would be $5 billion divided by 5 million, or $1,000 per rider. Critics would argue that a taxi, even a Beverly Hills taxi, would charge much less than $1,000 per ride.

Of course I am partially kidding. There are environmental and congestion benefits from building such a subway, and the subway would live on for years. But transit advocates must admit that in the absence of huge federal subsidies of up to 80 percent, there would be a serious public policy debate over whether subways are a good investment of scarce tax dollars. The case for building such a costly subway would be stronger if the federal government taxed gasoline to reflect its contribution to climate change. One leading economics study concluded that the tax on gasoline should be $1 a gallon higher than it is today. If the average household consumes 700 gallons of gasoline a year, this extra $700-a-year tax on gasoline expenditure would push some of them to switch from using their cars to taking public transit.

## Could Public Transit Become Hip in Los Angeles?

Ridership of a new subway would increase if LA's density increased to match a Manhattan-style density (via higher apartment buildings) on the west side of Los Angeles. Climate change will increase the demand to live closer to the temperate, low-smog coast. If in the near future the United States passes a carbon tax or cap and trade program for electricity consumption and fuel consumption, this will create incentives to live in high-density skyscrapers in West LA locations. In a nutshell, there will be incentives and infrastructure developed to make Los Angeles look more like Manhattan. Given that buildings can live for one hundred years, these changes to the city's urban form will only gradually be noticeable. Manhattan is the densest county in the United States, with an average of 70,595 residents per square mile. If parts of Los Angeles could achieve a similar density, this would create a market demand for fast subways that would be used and pay for themselves. In comparing the carbon footprint of the nation's major cities, New York City has a small footprint. This is due to its residents' use of public transit and living in relatively small homes. Given its temperate climate, West Los Angeles could have an even smaller footprint if people there lived at Manhattan's density.

Who might demand such new urbanist living? Crime in LA has been on the decline. In the past, suburbanization has been fueled by "flight from center city blight." But this process could reverse. Amenity-seeking young people and empty nesters enjoy the high quality of life in the center city. Households with young children would be less likely to demand such dense apartment living.

If Los Angeles starts to resemble Manhattan's urban form, it could help to reduce this city's notorious traffic congestion. A dense coastal core of high-rise buildings would provide a political constituency who might vote in favor of congestion pricing on LA's major highways.

Despite its well-known traffic congestion, Los Angeles has been slow to experiment with innovative solutions for this problem. In 2003 London implemented the Central London Congestion Charge.[23] Commuters pay a fee of roughly $15 when they enter the center city during peak times. The road charge could vary over the course of the day. At 3:00 A.M., when the roads are empty, the road charge could be zero. Such incentives would help to spread out driving over the course of the day, reducing demand at the peak and increasing demand off-peak. This would increase traffic speeds during rush hour. The revenue collected from such a program could be used to improve public transit. This is the approach that London has adopted. By improving basic bus service (in its frequency and the quality of a ride), London has managed to lure middle-class people to commute using this mode. As public transit is no longer viewed as a poor person's travel technology, any stigma effects vanish, and this further reinforces willingness to commute using public transit.

Outside of dense Northeastern cities such as New York City, Washington, D.C., and Boston, and environmentalist cities such as San Francisco, it is not a stretch to claim that the poor and lower middle class disproportionately commute using public transit. But this is not a constant. Improvement in the quality of public transit and densification would both reverse this long-term trend.

### Hurdles: Local Growth Controls

To protect LA residents from climate change, we want to encourage more dense development near the water in coastal communities such as Santa Monica, Venice, Malibu, and Pacific Palisades. These communities are cooler and face less smog than East Los Angeles. The densification of West LA would offer global carbon mitigation benefits.

But wealthy, coastal communities are likely to block new apartment towers. Local cities control land use and permitting for new construction. At least up to this point, these communities have not encouraged such high-density land use. There is a certain irony here. The residents of these communities are pro-green Prius drivers, eagerly installing solar panels on their houses' large roofs. On a day-to-day basis, they are living green and are proud of it. But Barbra Streisand and friends might not welcome thirty-story skyscrapers nearby. By giving their individual communities an implicit veto right on local development, Los Angeles as a metropolitan area loses access to a readily available adaptation strategy.

Consider Santa Monica and Beverly Hills, two beautiful cities located in West Los Angeles. Each has a population of roughly 90,000. Between 1990 and 2008, Beverly Hills averaged permitting 61 new total units per year, while Santa Monica issued new permits for 303 units per year. In this highly desirable community with roughly 30,000 housing units, this is a very small growth rate.

Some claim that the west side of Los Angeles has no land for development, but when I walk from Beverly Hills down Wilshire Avenue to UCLA, I see plenty of land parcels that could be converted from their current purposes into high-density housing. In pristine Santa Monica, I see one-story auto repair shops that could be torn down and built up into six-story buildings. If such a building had twelve new units that each sold for $1 million, then the total revenue from this conversion would be $12 million. Could the auto repair shop's present discounted value of its future profits really be close to $12 million? I don't think so. This suggests that binding zoning regulation is inhibiting the conversion of scarce land to its highest value use. This grosses out the economist, and it should also upset environmentalists who are eager to see Los Angeles be nimble enough to adapt to changing climate conditions.

### Sacrifice Golf to Save the People

West Los Angeles has other parcels of land that might be more desirable than converted commercial properties. Consider the private golf courses. These large green open spaces are reserved for wealthy golfers. I still like Tiger Woods, and I wish I was in as good physical condition as John Daly, but let's think about what developers could build on the combined prime land at just two golf courses on the west side. Together the Riviera Country Club and the Los Angeles Country Club take up 377 acres (0.6 square mile) of prime West LA real estate. If the land were built up at Manhattan's density of 70,595 people per square mile, it would yield housing for $0.6 \times 70{,}595 = 42{,}357$ people. If on average there are three people to an apartment unit, then 14,119 new housing units could be built there. If each sells for $1 million, the total new real estate would be worth roughly $14 billion. The increase in supply would cause the price of nearby housing to fall, but this negative supply effect is unlikely to be large. There are a number of people around the world eager to live the West LA lifestyle. Yes, there are tradeoffs. I am sacrificing golf for shrinking our per capita footprint and adapting to climate change. But such densification would create a virtuous cycle, as it would increase the demand and usage of a Wilshire subway. This "Manhattanization" of the west side would offer a variety of medium- and long-term environmental benefits. If West Los Angeles does become more amenable to high-density development, there are also fundamental engineering challenges that will have to be addressed. As everyone knows, Los Angeles is prone to earthquakes. Building tall buildings in earthquake zones poses a set of engineering challenges that would have to be tackled.

Readers who love golf may now view me as the great Satan. I apologize for infringing on your constitutional right to play golf in paradise. My real goal here is to encourage a reconsideration of current land use regulations in Los Angeles. With such relatively small changes to status quo policies, this city can make a big push toward achieving a sustainable future in a hotter world.

## Prices Matter

A major theme in this chapter has been the importance of getting prices right in our hotter future. I am not talking about Starbucks but rather about basic necessities such as electricity and water. Climate change will simultaneously increase the demand for them while restricting their supply. A consistent irony is that government policy is hindering urban adaptation to climate change. Up to this point, local and federal government policies have not helped our cities prepare for climate change. In both water pricing and electricity pricing, by placing a ceiling on prices and introducing strange implicit subsidies (such as the one directed toward Candy Spelling's property), Los Angeles and other major cities are choosing not to expose urbanites to real scarcity signals. Los Angeles is risking its green future by its continued mispricing of scarce resources.

My city is not alone in this regard. Similar policies are in place in many U.S. cities. Capped prices matter because many of us need an explicit nudge to change our ways. Behavioral economists emphasize that like Homer Simpson, we are lazy procrastinators. But if we are serious about making a proactive push to adapt to climate change, we must face the truth about rising scarcity in our hotter world.

As an LA homeowner with a big mortgage, I need to believe that Los Angeles has a bright future. But it will continue to compete with other superstar cities. Will Dodgers' manager Joe Torre regret having moved from New York City to LA? Everything in life is relative, so let's turn to New York City to see what curve balls climate change will throw to Yankee Derek Jeter and his friends in the Big Apple.

# 5
# WILL MANHATTAN FLOOD?

y parents, who live in Manhattan, go bird watching in Central Park; some New Yorkers jog on river paths, and they certainly sun themselves when the weather finally turns pleasant. But most New Yorkers spend most of their time inside, insulated from summer heat and winter cold. Manhattan is filled with rich people who escape the summer humidity by retreating to vacation areas. In midsummer, Manhattan feels nearly deserted. You can even get into the fancy restaurants in August. Everyone has left for the Hamptons, and some have gone to France. If climate change turns up the heat, then the wealthy will spend even less time hanging around the city during summer.

But of course there is more to New York City than Manhattan. My grandfather lived in Rego Park, Queens, for many years. Many of his neighbors in the outer boroughs do not have the money or free time to escape the heat. In our hotter future, they will crank up their air conditioning to cope. With millions of people simultaneously seeking such relief, the demands on the region's power grid will be huge. Siting such power-generating capacity in the densely populated NIMBY Northeast will be quite a challenge.

There is a certain irony that New York City could be hit quite hard by climate change. Relative to other cities such as Houston, New York has a small carbon footprint. It features the highest rate of public transit use in the United States, and it has the highest population density in the nation. On a typical day, most Manhattan residents do not set foot in an automobile or enter a single-family McMansion. They are living a life that our Western European green friends would not sneer at.

### Increased Danger in the Big City

On a day-to-day basis, New York will not be greatly affected by climate change, although climate forecasters are predicting that New York's already icky humid summers will become somewhat nastier. Between 1971 and 2000, New York averaged fourteen days a year over 90 degrees F. Mean annual temperatures are projected by global climate models to increase by roughly 2 degrees F by the 2020s and by 4 to 8 degrees F by the 2080s.[1] But climate change could have a different kind of severe effect on New York and cities like it.

In the movie *Armageddon*, Bruce Willis, Billy Bob Thornton, and Ben Affleck teamed up as astronauts to save the earth from an approaching giant asteroid. Such an asteroid is a "fat tail" risk. There is a very low probability that it would hit the earth—but if it did, it would be deadly. Climate change raises the likelihood that nasty climate-related events will take place, but the risk is ambiguous and difficult to quantify. Although it is easy to sketch possible future nasty scenarios, we simply do not know how much damage New York City would suffer from such an event. Climate modelers can confidently state that there is a "fat tail" risk of scenario x or scenario y taking place, but they cannot quantify it in a satisfying way to make a definite statement such as, "The risk of such a disastrous flood was 1 in 5 million and now due to climate change is 1 in 100,000."

Unquantified risk can be difficult to deal with, and New York is filled with risk-averse people. Woody Allen is known to have a range of phobias any one of which could earn a lot of Scrabble points (claustrophobia, cynophobia, acrophobia, carcinophobia, enochlophobia).[2] As climate change brews, Woody is likely to suffer from a severe case of the newly diagnosed floodophobia (or antlophobia). He will not be alone.

Some will shrug and say, as Frank Sinatra sang, "New York, New York." But the many phobics will worry about what their New York future has in store for them. People differ with respect to how much they fear uncertainty. For generations, my family has invested its money in treasury bonds and bank certificates of deposit insured by the federal government—low-yield, low-risk investments. For reasons I cannot explain, we are wimps who prefer a sure, low rate of return on our investments to a more volatile portfolio that offers a higher rate of return. We have paid a price for our unwillingness to be bold. Historically (but not during the 2000s), the stock market has offered a 7 percent annual rate of return over the long haul. At that rate, a dollar invested now will double in value in roughly eleven years.

We Kahns never go to Las Vegas, but there are plenty of other people who love to gamble and take risks, ranging from bungee jumping to motorcycling without a helmet. If there is general consensus about the risks that Manhattan faces, these are the types of people who will start to migrate there. Alternatively, if there is disagreement about the risks that climate change poses to Manhattan, then over time the most optimistic people (those who do not believe the threat is real) and the daredevils will both be found in increasing numbers.

To remain in Manhattan is to take a gamble when we really do not know the probability of certain scary scenarios occurring. Contrast this with playing lotto. By law, we are told what the probability of winning is and how much money we will receive if we do win.[3] Such information is useful for knowing whether this is a good game to play. Climate change risks are not unique to New York City. Cities such as Boston, London, and Singapore face similar challenges.

What kinds of ambiguous risks will New Yorkers face? Climate modelers are most worried about a "triple witching hour," in which climate change raises sea levels and then a major hurricane occurs during high tide. The geographical facts are clear. Manhattan is surrounded by water: the Atlantic, Long Island Sound, and the Hudson, Harlem, and East rivers. Ten percent of the city's land mass, including much of Lower Manhattan and the city's three airports, is less than three meters above sea level.[4]

Climate change will cause an unknown amount of sea level rise. Given the city's precarious geography, this could inflict scary losses on it. Imagine if southern Manhattan were flooded. As a writer in *Walrus* magazine put it,

> The subway system would become unusable. Sewage treatment plants would experience reverse flow leading waste in their pipes to be pushed back to the origins of apartment building basements. Hundreds of combined sewer outflows embedded in seawalls line the city's extensive shoreline, and if water levels spike, these pipes could be abruptly inundated, resulting in a massive flow of contaminated backwash into countless basements. New York's transit infrastructure is even more at risk, because so much of it is already below sea level.[5]

Subway flooding can cripple the city—and has. Each day the New York subway is the key transportation mode for getting people around the city.[6] Recent storms provide a preview of how climate change will affect the city. "In 2004, torrential downpours associated with Hurricane Frances inundated the city with more than two inches of rain an hour," reported the *New York Times'* city room blog:

> Hundreds of thousands of commuters were stranded. As rain-water seeps through tunnel walls and flows down subway grates and stairwells, sump pumps in 280 pump rooms next to the sub-way tracks pull the water back up to street level. That water then naturally flows toward the storm drains—but the storm drains themselves are often unable to handle the flow of water. Most of New York City's 6,000 miles of sewage lines are dual use; they handle rain runoff as well as sewage and industrial waste-water in the same pipes, before delivering the mixture to the city's 14 wastewater treatment plants. Heavy rains perennially overwhelm the pipes, causing the flow to back up, dumping everything from fecal matter and household trash to industrial pollutants like oil, grease and heavy metals into the city's water-ways and streets.[7]

When treatment plants are swamped, the excess spills from 490 overflow pipes throughout the city's five boroughs. Yuck.

### Planning Ahead to Avoid Risk Posed by Climate Change

New York is an old city with buildings and basic infra-structure (like its water systems and subway system) that were built long ago. An optimist would hope that although New York has relatively little new construction, such new construction will be built to last for one hundred years or so and be able to withstand the likely blows that climate change has in store for us. Surely moving forward we will build to be prepared?

The news is mixed. In the case of subway improvements, as the city builds new stations and updates the system, it is preparing for some of climate change's impacts. New subway entrances and exits are at least ten feet above the flood line established by the Federal Emergency Management Agency (FEMA). Passengers entering the Second Avenue line, for example, will have to walk up a little before they walk down. New stations will also be more flood-proof because they won't allow as much water to come in from the street as do the older stations.[8]

But consider Columbia University's major new Manhattanville Project. This construction project will lead to a new campus in the Manhattanville section of West Harlem:

> When completed, it will transform 17 acres in West Harlem into a modern, academic mixed–use development with 6.8 million square feet of new state-of-the-art facilities that will help solidify New York City as a world-renowned center for higher education and scientific research and enhance New York's ability to attract highly-skilled talent. In addition to creating a projected 14,000 construction jobs over the course of the 25-year build-out and 6,000 permanent jobs, the expansion will provide nearly 100,000 square feet of publicly accessible open space, enhance the area's cultural activities, and activate the neighborhood's street life with wide sidewalks and ground-floor retail uses.[9]

Columbia University is one of the top U.S. research universities. Its world-famous Earth Institute is home to dozens of prominent climate change scientists. If any institution in New York is going to "walk the walk" when it comes to preparing for climate change, it would be Columbia, right? Before answering that question, I must admit up front that I was a faculty member at Columbia for seven happy years until I moved to Boston in 2000, where I lived for another seven years (then moved to Los Angeles in early 2007).

Columbia University geophysicist Klaus Jacob is one of the world's leading experts on the causes and consequences of urban environmental disasters. He is also a graduate of Columbia. Like a modern-day Nostradamus, he has a nasty vision of a possible future involving the new Columbia campus, and he has tried to influence the course of history by conveying his concerns to university officials so that they will consider building a safer campus that can withstand the climate risk that he foresees.

The *Village Voice* has reported, "Expansion plans call for the largest underground complex in the city, a massive, 80-foot-deep basement that will extend only a block from the banks of the Hudson River. That's an underground space large enough to hold an eight-story building, lying only a few hundred feet from water that's susceptible to storm surge."[10]

Jacob's nightmare scenario involves a climate change–induced increase in the number of Category 2 hurricanes, with 110-mile-an-hour winds slamming the city. As the Hudson River rises by 10 feet, there will be vast flooding of the Manhattanville Campus. Sprawling labs that contain bio-hazards will flood, and some of these materials will seep out into the water and spread across neighborhoods.[11]

Jacob is concerned that Columbia's building plans do not take into account climate change's new risks at all. He worries that the new campus is directly in a flood zone. Because no-body at Columbia has taken his concerns seriously, he has launched a public relations media campaign that was written up in the *Village Voice* in the fall of 2008. Columbia's officials wrote him off as a "Chicken Little" and a pest. He has voiced his disappointment that Columbia, at least up to this point, is not setting an example by "practicing what it preaches" and backing up its sustainability research efforts by being a leader in day-to-day adaptation efforts.[12]

Columbia has countered that its new campus does not face serious risk. As evidence it points to FEMA flood maps, but the irony here is that these maps were last updated in 1983. The whole point of a research university is to create new knowledge. As the world's climate changes, leading re-searchers seek to be ahead of the curve and provide a heads-up to policy makers so that they can make informed choices about irreversible investments of billions of dollars in projects such as the Manhattanville Project. Climate change means that tomorrow will not look like yesterday. Columbia Univer-sity officials are implicitly assuming that climate change has not changed the objective risks that their new campus will face. This could be a very costly miscalculation.

The university is not denying that climate change is coming, but it is making an implicit bet. It is taking a "wait and see" position. Today, it would be costly to build in the safeguards that Klaus Jacob wants to minimize flood risk. Columbia is betting that over time it will have new information (based on climate modeling) about how big a threat sea level rise really is. It is betting that when this new information arrives, it can "reoptimize" and move biohazards out of basements that could flood, as well as that at some future point it could invest in cheaper defense as engineers make progress and the world as a whole demands more antiflooding products. Whether this is a risky bet or not is an open question. I can certainly imagine that Columbia's accountants are not eager to spend a lot of money now to fight a risk that they think will unfold in the distant future and may not occur at all. But this story highlights the fundamental challenge in making proactive investments. If a progressive institution, featuring liberal intellectual leaders such as Jeff Sachs and Joe Stiglitz, is unwilling to make proactive investments, can we be confident that Wall Street's "Masters of the Universe" will take any steps at all? In fairness, the strategy of delaying costly action makes sense if we are highly confident that climate change's impacts will be gradual.

## Mayor Bloomberg Looks into the Future

Extremely dangerous, unlikely events pose a major challenge to urban politicians. If they do nothing, it is likely that nothing bad will happen; 99.999 percent of the time, taxpayer money devoted to other urban issues such as public education will not have been wasted on "climate proofing" the city. If the mayor takes costly action such as zoning off development on land at risk or investing in enormously expensive defensive engineering projects, and then Mother Nature chooses not to storm the area, the politician will be accused of being a "Chicken Little" and wasting taxpayer money.

The mayor of New York City is aware of the challenge of forecasting climate change's impacts. The Bloomberg administration has commissioned a set of experts to identify what the most likely future climate scenarios are. Mayor Bloomberg has convened the New York City Panel on Climate Change (NPCC), which consists of leading climate change and impact scientists, academics, and private-sector practitioners. It is charged with advising the mayor and the New York City Climate Change Adaptation Task Force on issues related to climate change and adaptation as it relates to infrastructure.[13]

The Bloomberg administration has called for new flood-zone maps in its PlaNYC 2030 project, the mayor's much-touted, long-term sustainability plan. That initiative calls for maps that would take global climate change into account, as well as changes in the building code to match.[14]

I am impressed that Mayor Bloomberg is taking such a long-term perspective. He is unlikely to still be mayor in 2070. Although he is a Manhattan property owner, his property is near Central Park and is unlikely to face flooding risk. Politicians are often accused of having a short-term perspective as they seek out policies that raise their reelection prospects.

With the typical voter focused on crime, school quality, and whether the New York Yankees will remain in the Bronx, it takes a special politician to embrace such a long-term outlook.

Mike Bloomberg is not your typical mayor. He became a billionaire by creating a company (Bloomberg Inc.) that collects information and distributes it to Wall Street traders. He is well aware of the value of information in helping decision makers to make better long-term decisions. It must frustrate him that the leading experts on climate change cannot provide him with precise predictions about how and when climate change will strike.

It is unknown whether Bloomberg's example will spur other coastal mayors (such as the mayor of Boston) to engage in similar projects investigating specific long-term predictions for their cities. Some mayors may view climate change as taking place way after their term ends, while others may view such an "impact assessment" as a waste of money. Similar to New York City, London is currently investigating how it will be affected by climate change. Its analysis reveals that it is at risk from the urban heat island effect and the likely increased risk of flooding of the Thames River. Unlike New York City, it is also worried about its water supplies, as it recognizes that its water supply per person today is similar to Israel's.[15]

The New York mayor's project has yielded consensus climate predictions concerning how *average* temperature, rainfall, and sea level rise will be affected by the end of the twenty-first century. But in addressing the big issue of adapting to climate change, the average risk is less important than the "fat tails." Given the enormous possible losses associated with Manhattan flooding, we really care about what the likelihood of a major flood sometime in the next one hundred years is and how much damage to life and property this would cause. Climate modelers are producing topographical maps highlighting geographical areas at risk under various climate scenarios. The U.S. Army Corps of Engineers estimates that if a Category 3 hurricane hit New York, nearly 30 percent of the south side of Manhattan would be flooded.[16]

## Would Threats to Manhattan Weaken the New York Economy?

There is nothing inherently productive about Manhattan. Its soil and climate do not foster productivity. Despite these facts, it attracts the very best lawyers, doctors, financial experts, and executives in many fields. It is a productive place because of the select set of superstars who choose to work there. Nobel Laureate Thomas Schelling was the first to sketch the basic focal point story: Tomorrow you have to meet a stranger in New York City. Where and when do you meet the person? This is a coordination game. There are many possible outcomes. Schelling asked a group of students this question and found the most common answer was "at noon at (the information booth at) Grand Central Station." There is nothing that makes "Grand Central Station" a "correct answer" due to some intrinsic value of being there, but it is a traditional meeting place that is commonly known. So I know that you know that I know that this is a typical meeting place.

Manhattan acts as a similar magnet. Unlike in the Grand Central Station scenario, firms make their locational decisions at staggered points in time. Great companies such as Goldman Sachs and NBC have established offices in New York. New companies can locate nearby with confidence that they will have access to these giants. But just because these leading companies have been in Manhattan doesn't mean that they will always remain in New York City. If these anchor firms move on, they could set off a domino effect.

Wall Street is Manhattan's major growth engine. Finance-related business generates a huge amount of income tax revenue for the city and state. If Manhattan does face serious climate change risk, the finance industry can respond to this change by moving away from southern Manhattan. If it simply moves to higher ground in Queens, then New York State will not lose tax revenue from this geographical move. However, Wall Street was leaving Wall Street even before the terrorist attacks of 9/11/2001.

New York City has a highly undiversified economy relying on finance, the media, hospitals, and tourism. During the deep recession of 2009, the city was reminded that it booms and busts with Wall Street's fortunes. Although heat waves are unlikely to scare off too many tourists, the risk of flooding and fears of disruption may accelerate the migration of financial jobs to "higher ground" in New Jersey and New York City suburbs.

In the face of climate change, the New York metropolitan area will continue to thrive even if parts of Manhattan suffer. Climate change will threaten southern Manhattan and Long Island with flood risk, but much of the suburbs will "merely" suffer from extended heat waves in the face of climate change. Given its geography, Manhattan faces more risk than the boring suburban communities in New Jersey and Westchester. It is quite possible that because of climate change, specific locations in New York City will lose employment while others will gain employment.

Hedge funds now trade from posh suburban neighborhoods such as Greenwich, Connecticut. Back-office finance jobs have been migrating to cheaper-rent areas in New Jersey and outside of Manhattan. There is no doubt that big deals and power lunches will continue to take place, but there is no guarantee that they will take place in southern Manhattan. If this part of Manhattan becomes uninhabitable, then other parts of the metropolitan area that are viewed as "climate safe" will gain. The borough of Queens could receive a makeover. Yes, planes fly over constantly as they approach JFK and LaGuardia airports, but such easy access to airports and to Mets games could be viewed as an amenity. Technological advance is even muffling airport noise. The new generation of jet planes is much quieter than earlier vintages.

Wall Street firms are mobile, but the city's universities and hospitals are less so. Columbia and New York University cannot get up and go. This fact should provide some assurance for Manhattan's landowners that there will continue to be major employers who are tied to this specific piece of real estate. These employers act as a credible anchor, guaranteeing that the skilled will continue to work downtown.

## Who Suffers from Climate Change?

In the New York metro area, the rich, the middle class, and the poor will feel different impacts caused by climate change. Rich people tend to be landowners. A Donald Trump owns valuable pieces of land on the best streets of Manhattan. During good times, such as when Wall Street is booming, the Donald becomes even richer. But the reverse is also true. Bad "new news" about Manhattan's future quality of life will make his hair do even wilder things. How his asset position is affected by this news hinges on where within the city his properties are located. If southern Manhattan becomes quite risky due to climate change and everyone knows about this new risk, then its land values will decline.

Middle-class renter households will feel climate change's impact in daily life. Insights into the quality-of-life impacts of increased storms are offered by the *New York Post*:

Letters from the New York Post[17]

DOES THE 'M' IN MTA STAND FOR 'MORONIC'?
August 12, 2007
THE ISSUE: Wednesday's storm and the ensuing MTA challenges.

As we spend countless hours and dollars to make ourselves more secure against the threat of terrorism, it seems that such minor infrastructure problems are more likely to gravely affect the lives of everyday New Yorkers.

When will our elected leaders see that if rain can virtually cripple a great metropolis like New York, these mass-transit and utility problems have moved beyond the realm of minor problems into major ones?

We expect New York to be great, yet our increasing number of infrastructure failures is slowly making us resemble a regrettable backwater unworthy of the nickname the Empire State.

—Kathy B. Huang, Manhattan

*******

Why are we paying and, more to the point, trusting the MTA to expand the transit system when it can't operate what it has?

As it contemplated new subway lines and cathedral-like stations, one of the seasoned executives, expert study groups or high-priced consultants might have realized that New York is subject to the occasional summer thunderstorm.

Why can't we spend some money on fixing the storm drains?

Just because the MTA has problems getting work done, it shouldn't mean the rest of us can't get to work.

—Michael Duff, Queens

*******

These letters reveal the frustration that normal New Yorkers feel as their day-to-day routine is impinged upon. These writers are shocked that an "obvious problem" (that it can rain heavily) has not been addressed by one of the world's richest and most sophisticated cities. This city that depends on public transportation does not offer a diversified set of transit options. You can walk or take the subway, the bus, or a private taxi. But for most commutes within the city, the first is impractical and the last is too expensive, and the bus is slow and infrequent. Unlike other cities where people can use private vehicles, New Yorkers depend on the subway system to operate.

These people do not want to hear excuses about the city's old infrastructure and about slow progress in renovating it. They want this problem to vanish. They must have assumed that the city had recognized this problem and was working on a solution. These nasty floods are relatively rare events—for now—and there is no way for the average Joe to know if the system is now stress ready.

Despite gentrification, southern Manhattan is home to a diverse population. A swelling Chinatown is home to more than 100,000 people. Many of these households are living in high-density apartments and many are poor immigrants. They are likely to bear the major costs of adapting to climate change. This group doesn't own second homes or powerful air conditioning to fend off climate change's impacts during summer heat waves and on elevated air pollution days.

New York City is a major destination for specific immigrant groups such as Haitians and people from Puerto Rico and the Dominican Republic. Immigrants choose destinations where they know people who have previously settled there. As I discuss in a later chapter, climate change is likely to have major impacts on developing countries and poorer regions. This will create a large flow of environmental refugees. New York is likely to become home to a growing number of these displaced immigrant households. As these households seek jobs and apartments, the standard of living for the urban poor in the city will fall. Low-skill wages will fall, and rents will rise. Cross-group residential community clashes could arise as the growing immigrant population crosses previous ethnic borders in the greater boroughs such as the Bronx, Brooklyn, and Queens.

Neighborhoods in New York are always changing. When my grandfather first came to the United States in 1926, he lived in southern Manhattan. Southern Manhattan has traditionally been an employment center revolving around Wall Street, but this has changed over time. As Wall Street has left Wall Street, much of this land is turning into residential neighborhoods. "Lower Manhattan is the fastest-growing residential area in the city right now," said outgoing Economic Development Corporation president Andrew Alper. "It will go from 23,000 residents to 46,000—double—by 2008. By 2030, the number we are using is roughly 80,000 people. That's a pretty good-sized city in most parts of the world."[18]

In terms of protecting the populace from climate change risk, this is an ominous trend. As more people live downtown, they will have greater congressional representation and mayoral support to protect their communities. Ideally, this will strengthen their communities. Unfortunately, just as officials in Venice may deny the effects of climate change in an effort to boost the reputation of their city, local boosters in New York may argue that climate change poses no threats as they try to continue to attract new families to move there. This suppression of evidence can have a lulling effect and lead too many people to locate in a risky area. The problem is that climate shocks are still rare events. An area may enjoy ten good years of no flooding, and people will optimistically conclude that the area faces no risk. But this is equivalent to extrapolating that Shaquille O'Neal will make 100 percent of his free throws after watching him make his first ten in a new season.

## Magic Bullets and Technological Fixes

Engineers and politicians are discussing a variety of ambitious engineering schemes to protect coastal cities from rising sea levels. Singapore offers a poignant case study of the power of engineering measures. Singapore is vulnerable to climate change. Much of the island is less than 15 meters above sea level, with a generally flat coast. With a population of about 4.7 million within its 193-kilometer coastline, Singapore is one of the most densely populated countries in the world. Since 1991 the Public Utilities Board (PUB) has required new reclamation projects to be built to 125 centimeters above the highest recorded tide level. The state has invested a large amount of money (over $230 million) to complete the

Marina Barrage. The Marina Barrage is part of a comprehensive flood control scheme to alleviate flooding in the low-lying areas of the city. The Barrage will separate the seawater from the freshwater and act as a tidal barrier to keep out the high tides.[19] London has made similar investments:

> While London had been building up the embankments along the Thames since the late nineteenth century, the 1953 storm galvanized Westminster to ensure that Britain's first city was adequately protected. It took thirty years to build the Thames Flood Barrier, a 520-metre safety valve located about five kilometres east of the Isle of Dogs. Clearly visible in satellite photographs, the barrier consists of nine conch-shaped piers, between which swivel twenty-meter-high, steel-plated flood-gates. Engineered to withstand a storm that would only be likely to occur once in 1,000 years.[20]

New York City faces similar threats. Some experts are already proposing to build enormous, retractable storm surge barriers in three locations around New York, including one straddling the Verrazano Narrows and another at Throgs Neck, where Long Island Sound meets the East River. Such barriers, rising 15 meters above sea level, would effectively wall off New York Harbor if a major hurricane sent tsunami-like waves toward the city.[21]

Such technological optimism can actually increase the amount of damage that climate change imposes on New York City. This boomerang effect can occur if blind faith in technological fixes lulls the public into a false sense of security.

Imagine an extreme case in which Donald Trump Jr. builds an expensive new condominium complex in part of southern Manhattan, discounting the risk because he is convinced that the engineers have figured out how to protect the area from flooding. Suppose he, and the people who will buy his condos, believe that the risk of a true disaster is one in a million, but the truth is that there is a one in twenty chance of disaster. In this case, false faith in the engineers will raise the chance of a calamity. Trump will build an expensive tower. Very rich people will live there and will suffer greatly when the unexpected shock hits. This sad story could have been avoided if the rich didn't trust the engineers or had their own ability to figure out the "true" probability of a disaster. As in the Ponzi scheme that Bernard Madoff perpetrated, people are less likely to be victims if they engage in due diligence beforehand.

Engineers face the challenge that the public wants "magic bullet" solutions. We do not want to abandon the southern tip of Manhattan. If there are engineers who promise "solutions," urban politicians will have a stake in giving them a green light. I do not mean to imply that urban politicians are corrupt and willing to sacrifice their own constituents to keep power. Instead, I would push the wimpier claim that it is human nature to protect your turf by engaging in wishful thinking (that the risk isn't real or can be solved through a technological fix). Historically unique, at-risk cities are unlikely to simply surrender to climate change. Their citizens can move to higher ground, but they cannot themselves get up and go. Their boosters will fight hard to make the case that these cities can continue to thrive in a hotter world. A tragedy could occur if politicians seeking to encourage the growth of their own jurisdictions provide a public seal of approval to engineering projects that they are not qualified to evaluate. In this case, innocent residents who trust the politicians will choose to live in areas that expose them to great risk from climate change.

Such suckering can always take place. We often find ourselves in situations where we must trust an expert and make a decision (such as where to live or how to repair a used car), aware that we do not fully know all the facts about the situation. In the case of a medical diagnosis or a broken car, we can always get a second opinion. But in the case of judging whether an area is at significant risk of climate change and figuring out whether engineering fixes are sufficient to mitigate the risk, I doubt that a correct diagnosis can be made. The boosters will say that everything is fine, but they could be lying or blissfully unaware of the new risks that climate change poses. A risk-averse household would respond by living somewhere else in the metropolitan area, but there are plenty of risk lovers and middle-class households looking for real estate bargains. They will want to believe that the engineers can deliver on their promises.

Manhattan could empower the insurance market and the land use regulators to take steps to help the city adapt. Enforcing zoning codes and allowing "price gouging" insurance pricing would put both fewer residences and jobs in harm's way. Zoning codes could be used to discourage new development in the areas of southern Manhattan that are at greatest risk from flooding. The current owners of the land would become worse off because demand for their scarce asset would decrease. Insurance pricing differentials would also discourage certain types of economic activity in flood zones. Suppose that insurance premiums could freely float based on the fundamentals of supply and demand rather than being capped by government regulation. If actuaries assess that a given parcel of land is at significant flood risk, then for-profit insurers would only sell an insurance premium for such a property at a very high price. This would send a sharp price signal to businesses, discouraging them from locating in flood areas. This differential insurance pricing might appear to discriminate, but life insurance companies already do so, charging smokers and nonsmokers different rates for insurance. This spatially differentiated pricing policy would force all businesses and households to think through whether locating in southern Manhattan is right for them. Unlike a zoning code, which would target only new construction, such insurance pricing might even push some southern Manhattan firms to move to safer ground.

## Paying for a Good Defense

Chapter 2 presented the case that individual cities should be paying for the bulk of their own defense against climate change's impacts. Local police and fire services are paid for from local revenues; climate change adaptation expenditures represent a similar investment. If a city's residents were all homeowners, such owners would recognize that their homes will be more valuable if the city is perceived to be safe from new climate change risk. We all know that homes in high-crime areas sell for a price discount. This same logic implies that homes in areas at risk from flooding will also sell for a discount.

A self-interested homeowner will vote in favor of climate adaptation strategies such as raising taxes to pay for public infrastructure, for example a sea wall, if the cost (his or her share of the tax bill) is less than the expected benefit. The benefit of such an investment is that it lowers the probability of a major flood, and this risk mitigation will be reflected in the resale value of the home.

But New York City, like Washington, D.C., San Francisco, and San Diego, is a renter city. In 2000 more than 50 percent of households in the whole metropolitan area of New York were renters. Homeowners and renters have different voting incentives. Suppose that a selfish renter only cares about paying a cheap monthly rent for her apartment. She should vote for having no police at all. Crime would rise in such communities, and as word spread to other cities that New York City is not safe, outsiders would be less interested in moving there. This reduction in demand would ultimately translate into reduced rental prices. By sacrificing quality of life, the renter lowers her rental payments! The homeowner has the opposite viewpoint. Like a shareholder of a company, the homeowner's asset (her home) is more valuable if the city is more desirable. Cities whose voters are mostly renters have less of an incentive to pay high taxes in return for investments for protecting the city. In a nutshell, they are not stakeholders in the city's future. If the city goes to hell, they can get up and go.

Both the owners and renters in New York City will hope that the federal government will pay for the bulk of any engineering "solutions" for defending Manhattan. As we collectively get ready to combat the effects of climate change, suppose that the United States keeps subsidizing coastal infrastructure protection. In this case, coastal cities will import transfers from inland "safe cities" such as Fargo, North Dakota. The kind people of Fargo will face higher taxes to pay for government expenditure that does not directly benefit them. Don Trump will e-mail them a thank-you note.

The people of Fargo would wish that Manhattan would do a better job protecting itself from increased flood risk. They would write to the New York City zoning commission encouraging it to improve its mapping capability to pinpoint the micro-flood zones within the city and encourage the city to reduce housing construction and density in those locations. Such precautionary investments would help to sharply reduce the damage that natural disasters cause.

Without federal funding, New York's climate adaptation expenditures would have to be financed with new revenues or by reducing other expenditures (such as garbage collection). In this case, a New York City mayor would have to convince the renter populace that a tax increase to improve the city's infrastructure will make everyone better off. Self-interested renters would have an incentive to vote against this. Why? Voting yes will raise their taxes in the short run and their rents in the long run (assuming they do not have a rent-controlled apartment). Yes, they would gain the climate-"proofing" benefits, but their direct out-of-pocket costs might exceed those anticipated gains. In contrast, homeowners would be much more likely to support this project because their asset (Manhattan real estate) is more valuable if Manhattan is perceived to be "climate-proofed."

This chapter has focused on both the day-to-day challenges that climate change will pose for New York City and the low-probability, high-risk scenarios that this Superstar city will face in the near future. New York's problems resemble the challenges that other leading coastal cities such as Boston, London, Hong Kong, and Shanghai will all face in grappling with our hotter world.

Although New York City resembles two of China's super-star cities in some ways, China is significantly poorer than the United States, has a very different political structure, and is currently experiencing much greater economic growth. I now turn to discussing how its cities will cope with climate change.

# 6

# WILL CHINA'S CITIES GO GREEN?

ince September 2006, Google China has been headquartered in a ten-story building near the fourth western ring road of Beijing, roughly 8 miles northwest of Tiananmen Square. The location is surrounded by bigger buildings housing clusters of high-tech firms filled with young workers. In September 2009 I spent two weeks in a hotel across the street from Google China. Although I am "only" forty-four, I felt like an old man because the happy workers in this high-tech cluster were in their twenties and early thirties. This employment center is very close to Tsinghua University's Southern Gate. Tsinghua is known as "China's

MIT" (that is, tech oriented and filled with lots of super-smart and tech-savvy pranksters), and the high-tech cluster's proximity to campus is no accident. I asked a 2000 graduate of Tsinghua University about the recent economic development in this high-tech area, and she told me that just ten years earlier this vibrant center had been vacant green fields.

Continuing this trend of turning green fields into concrete and glass, China is planning to create twenty new cities in each of the next twenty years.[1] Chairman Mao would certainly not recognize China's major cities today: Shanghai's skyline resembles Manhattan's. Today 10,000 new vehicles a week are being registered in Beijing.

China will soon be the world's major producer of greenhouse gas emissions. When confronted with this fact, China counters that it is a developing country whose current per capita carbon emissions are roughly one-fifth as much as per capita U.S. emissions. So there. But critics reply that its population is more than four times larger than that of the United States, and its annual 8 percent real per capita income growth is boosting its per capita emissions.

The Chinese government is focused on the goal of raising this nation's economic well-being—and not much on environmental effects. But such consequences are not fully understood. Scientists continue to debate whether the 2008 Sichuan earthquake that killed more than 80,000 people was caused by the construction and filling of the Zipingpu Dam.[2] Some scientists have conjectured that the 511-foot-high Zipingpu Dam, which holds 315 million tons of water, was sited too close to the fault line (just 550 yards away). "The scientists believe that the weight of water, and the effect of it penetrating into the rock, could have affected the pressure on the fault line underneath, possibly unleashing a chain of ruptures that led to the quake."[3] Although we don't know if all that water led to an earthquake, it is clear that reliance on industrial production and coal-fired power plants for electricity and heating have created some of the highest urban ambient particulate levels in the world. Numerous public health studies have documented the mortality effects of such elevated air pollution levels.

The recent Olympics in Beijing offer a possible optimistic preview of the future. Hoping that the marathon runners could thrive, or at least survive their 26.2-mile race during the 2008 Olympic Games in Beijing, the Chinese government enacted stringent regulations that reduced vehicle and industrial emissions. For example, whole factories were moved out of the city. Seventy percent of all government cars and vehicles owned by state-run enterprises were banned seven weeks ahead of the opening ceremony for the August 8–24 games.[4] This heavy-handed experiment worked. The Chinese authorities have claimed that air pollution decreased by roughly 50 percent because of this effort. Whether Beijing's growing middle and upper classes enjoyed their month of "clean air" and will now demand that their government enact regulations to maintain this level of air quality is an open question.

At the same time that China has the world's most polluted cities and is on its way to producing more greenhouse gas emissions than any other nation, it is choosing to become a leader in the production of the next generation of "green" products, which will create new export opportunities. In recent years China has emerged as a leading producer of hybrid and all-electric vehicles. In November 2009 the *China Daily News* reported that CSR Zhuzhou Electric Locomotive Co. will deliver light rail trains valued at 350 million yuan ($51.2 million) to Izmir City in Turkey in April 2012.[5] In the cities of Tangshan and Liaoyuan, new all-electric buses manufactured by China Lithium Energy Investment Group and Dongfeng Motor Corp. recently rolled off the production line and joined public transport systems. Equipped with 200 lithium batteries, an electric bus can travel 200 kilometers on a single charge. The government is offering a subsidy of roughly $80,000 per bus, which encourages local governments to purchase the "green" buses. The country's goal is to raise annual production capacity to 500,000 electric cars and buses by the end of 2011.[6]

Leading internationalists like *New York Times'* Tom Friedman are highly optimistic about China's "green" future.[7] In July 2009 Friedman speculated that China "will clean the U.S. clock" in competition over energy technology. He believes that China anticipates coming global energy scarcity and is wisely preparing to develop the next generation of energy-efficient products ready to export. He argues that China will "go green" not because of liberal environmentalism but in the hopes of seizing an emerging market. He writes, "China is increasingly finding that it *has to go green* out of necessity because in too many places, its people can't breathe, fish, swim, drive or even see because of pollution and climate change. Well, there is one thing we know about necessity: it is the mother of invention."[8]

This may be merely cheerleading and wishful thinking, but in Friedman's defense, he sketches a plausible future. He sees an entrepreneurial people eager to make money from the coming green wave. The Chinese premier has stated his intention to enact policies to sharply reduce his nation's energy intensity (energy consumption per dollar of gross domestic product, GDP), and the *China Daily News* devotes ample attention to the importance of the development of the "low-carbon" economy.

Hundreds of millions of people are moving to China's cities. Accommodating this growth requires enormous investment in everything it takes to have a well-functioning city. Sewer systems, power plants, highways, subways, office buildings, residential towers, and roads must all be built. Given that urban infrastructure, power plants, and buildings can live for fifty to one hundred years, the decisions made today and in the near future will have long-term consequences for how China's cities deal with climate change and carbon mitigation.

This continues a trend. Chinese cities have experienced dramatic income and population growth over the last thirty years, spurred by the inflow of foreign direct investment and privatization of state-owned enterprises. In turn, urban growth has fueled China's recent success.

The share of the population living in cities in China has increased from 28 percent in 1990 to 44 percent in 2006. The annual real income of an average urban resident in 2006 was four times higher than in 1990. The aggregate consequences of income growth can be seen in Beijing. In 2001 there were 1.5 million vehicles in Beijing. By August 2008 its vehicle count had grown to 3.3 million.

The Chinese government is well aware that it must manage the sharp growth of its economy and the rural-to-urban migration of hundreds of millions of people. Billions of dollars will be invested in the basic infrastructure of buildings, electric power generation, roads, subways, and sewer systems to cater to these new urbanites. All the capital in these growing cities, from the buildings to the sewer systems to the public transit systems, will be brand new. Newer capital tends to be cleaner and have embodied in it the best engineering practices. I saw this firsthand when I rode the Beijing subway. Although China is a developing country, the Beijing subway looked a lot better to me than rich New York City's old subways and subway stations. There are currently six subway lines operating in the city, and ten new lines under construction are slated to be completed by 2015. When completed, Beijing's rail network will constitute 350 miles of track. That compares favorably with LA's endless discussions of whether to build a 14-mile subway connecting downtown and my Westwood and running to the ocean, which at the earliest will be completed by 2036.[9]

Increasing labor mobility in urban China is pushing Chinese cities toward an open system. The binding "Hukou"—China's household residential registration system that restricts domestic migration—has weakened over time, which means that cities now have to compete with one another. As discussed in chapter 3, cross-city competition (through the tacit threat of out-migration) acts as a disciplining device for local politicians. If people can leave a city whose quality of life is declining (perhaps caused by climate change–induced shocks such as drought and floods), politicians have an incentive to set up contingency plans to help protect the public. A politician who fails to provide high-quality services will end up with a city bereft of skilled people.

## A Green City Future?

Chinese cities rank among the most polluted places in the world.[10] China is the largest source of $SO_2$ emissions in the world today, and the damage to health caused by air pollution cost China 3.8 percent of its GDP in 2007.[11] In 2006 Beijing's ambient air pollution (as measured by small particulate matter, PM10) was roughly four times higher than that in Los Angeles. But although China's local air pollution levels are high, they have declined in many cities recently.

In the United States over the last one hundred years, we have seen the transition of U.S. cities (think of New York City or Pittsburgh) from dirty producers to tourist-friendly green cities. Major cities in China may now be entering a similar transition.

Chinese demand for living in green cities will almost certainly rise as households become better educated and wealthier. Just as in other countries around the world, the footloose, skilled middle class will increasingly demand such amenities. In recent years China's universities have been graduating millions of students each year. What economists call "human capital"—the knowledge and skills of the population—is the most valuable asset a nation has. By enhancing local environmental quality in its major cities, China would protect the health of this precious asset. Education, wealth, and environmentalism go hand in hand. The better educated the population is, the more wealth it tends to generate, and the more it wants to live in green cities. More educated people are more likely to be environmentalists and thus favor adopting policies for protecting the environment.

In China's cities, households are revealing a taste for a clean environment. In my own research, I have compared the pricing of comparable apartment units (in Beijing no one lives in a single-family home) in clean and dirty parts of the city.[12] I have also made a similar comparison with other Chinese cities.[13] Both within Beijing and in other major cities, home prices are lower in communities and cities with higher ambient air pollution levels. Based on the U.S. experience, I predict that Chinese urbanites' willingness to pay for environmental protection will rise as the nation becomes richer.

Throughout the developed world, wealthier people have demanded more environmental protection as their nations have become richer. The U.S. Environmental Protection Agency (EPA) was founded in 1972—a surprisingly late birth date. The EPA's Clean Air Act has played an important role in reducing pollution in major U.S. cities. Regulation of new capital, ranging from new cars, to power plants, to industry has contributed to a significant improvement in public health due to decline in pollution. These gains have not been a free lunch. Some have claimed that regulation is a key reason for the U.S. economy's productivity slowdown in the 1970s. I don't believe this claim, but it is likely that American consumers have paid higher prices for final consumer products that embody regulated products such as electricity generated at coal-fired power plants and cars that have high-quality catalytic converters. Still, there has been little backlash against the Clean Air Act.

By developing later, China gets to learn from what the United States and Western Europe have done right and wrong. These free environmental policy lessons lower the price of achieving the win-win of growth and urban greenness. In 2000 China enacted its first emissions standards for new cars. Eight years later it adopted Europe's Euro IV vehicle emissions standards.[14] Although these standards only affect the emissions per mile from new vehicles, over time they will apply to more and more vehicles driving on Beijing's streets. Similar to California's experience, the gradual reduction in emissions per mile can offset increased miles driven, such that air pollution associated with transportation (such as ambient carbon monoxide) will improve even during a time of ongoing growth in Beijing and other major cities.

Technological breakthroughs such as environmental engineering techniques for lowering air pollution emissions from coal-fired power plants can be shared across nations. Such technological transfers open up the possibility of China's cities enjoying economic growth without the same environmental impacts that our cities suffered in the 1950s and 1960s. Growth economists have emphasized that we can all simultaneously gain from the spread of a good idea. In this sense, a good idea such as a new carbon mitigation strategy differs very much from a cheeseburger. When I eat the burger, you can't.

To overcome intellectual property issues, China has partnered with leading foreign companies to create joint ventures that help this nation import cutting-edge technology. General Motors first entered China in 1996, forming a partnership with Shanghai Automotive Industry Corp. In 2010 General Motors expects to sell 1.4 million vehicles (Chevrolets, Buicks, and Cadillacs) in China.[15]

This ongoing trend will reduce China's carbon intensity (emissions per dollar of output) and help it protect itself from climate change's impacts. In my own research, I have shown that foreign direct investment (FDI) inflows are helping to make Chinese cities cleaner as this investment leads cities to modernize their factories and invest in pollution control.[16] This finding counters a standard claim of environmentalists that international trade degrades environmental quality for poor countries. This pessimistic "pollution haven" logic argues that rich countries "outsource" their dirty activity to poor nations. Although international trade patterns in garbage and used durables—like old computers and cars—would support this claim, in the case of manufacturing, nations trade not only in goods but also in capital. Such capital flows from rich countries to poorer countries often have a beneficial environmental effect of modernizing production facilities.

## Growth and the Environment

Many environmentalists view economic growth and pollution production as synonyms. But economists argue that economic growth can trigger the production and consumption of higher-quality products that help to offset the pollution consequences of capitalism. After all, there are almost no zero-emissions hybrid vehicles (currently, the Prius is the only car that meets that definition) driving on the streets of Mumbai, but Berkeley, California, is filled with them. Yes, richer people have more income to purchase consumption goods, but this doesn't have to mean that they merely consume more. Such income also leads to higher-quality consumption and a greater willingness to spend money on the enforcement of environmental regulations. Ambient pollution is declining in several of China's growing cities, despite their relatively low level of income. If emissions per dollar of output can decline faster than economic output rises, then a growing nation can enjoy declining pollution.

## A Transition Tom Friedman Would Salute

China's coal-fired electric power plants are well-known major polluters. There are public health co-benefits from encouraging China to diversify its electric power generation. If China reduced its reliance on coal-fired electricity, this would simultaneously reduce its greenhouse gas emissions and its ambient air pollution. To quote Lau Nai-keung, a member of the Hong Kong Special Administrative Region Basic Law Committee of the National People's Congress Standing Committee:

> Recently on my way to Dunhuang, the Gansu city of caved Buddha fame, I was fascinated by what must be the largest wind farm on earth. These magnificent modern windmill arrays gently churned along both sides of the highway for miles forging a beautiful and highly unforgettable sight. Local officials later confirmed that this is the largest wind farm on earth, and it is situated in the city of Yumen, the first oil field in modern China. Its current capacity is 420,000 kilowatts, to be expanded by the year-end to 1 million kilowatts and ultimately to 10 million.
>
> This is the tip of the iceberg. Projects of similar size are now being commissioned in six clusters all over North China, and one along the coast of Zhejiang, with a total planned capacity approaching 120 million kilowatts. These wind farms have to be huge to meet the economic and stability requirements to join the national power grid. Wind energy is now part and parcel of the Chinese national power supply system. Wind energy is only part of the story. China is now leading the world in clean coal power plants, nuclear plant technology and is also the largest manufacturer of solar voltaic cells.[17]

Although there may be some nationalistic boosterism here, it is impressive that a developing nation with a major endowment of coal is actively seeking out a diversified low-carbon strategy for addressing its anticipated electricity needs. Such shifts in business-as-usual strategies of economic development are exactly what are needed to achieve the win-win of green growth.

## The Powerful State's Role in Climate Change Adaptation

In the midst of the H1N1 (swine flu) virus scare, the Chinese government has shown just how powerful it is. Potential entrants to the country are remotely scanned for signs of fever. Those who test positive are subsequently quarantined. Knowing that I am not a lucky guy, when I entered China in September 2009 I brought some extra reading and fun stuff to occupy my time in case I was sent to a hotel for two weeks of unexpected quarantine.

Although draconian and smacking of overkill, this reaction to the H1N1 flu highlights the Chinese government's capabilities and willingness to trade off individual freedoms for group protection. This might make a libertarian a bit queasy, but in the case of climate change adaptation, this muscular state will be able to achieve outcomes that the U.S. government cannot. Along other quality-of-life dimensions, the state has revealed a willingness to upgrade China's cities with actions such as antismoking laws, antispitting laws, and enforcement of both.

China's powerful government is pursuing a number of technological fixes to address the likely consequences of climate change. One prime example is investment in water desalinization.[18] If such technological investments pay off, China will simultaneously have effectively increased its water supply and be a step ahead in exporting this technology to nations suffering from drought under climate change.

A single-party state can pursue strong policies without having to wrestle the other political party or activist groups or face tough public criticism from opinion leaders such as the *New York Times*. The absence of checks and balances creates opportunities and challenges. An advantage for the autocratic state is that it can impose its will and make firm decisions. But by stifling open debate, the Communist Party may miss out on foreseeing the full consequences of important irreversible decisions.

## Playing Favorites

Until recently, China's development goals have centered on building up its coastal cities (such as Shanghai) with their access to the world export market, aiming to increase the nation's export capacity. To achieve this goal, the federal government has pursued a spatial favoritism strategy. This has meant that cities in the eastern region have received favorable fiscal and administration policies to help them grow first. The policy package includes tax reductions (business tax, company income tax, and other taxes) for foreign-invested companies and joint ventures, simplified examination and approval processes, and more infrastructure investment.

This plan has been successful to the point that it has produced significant inequality between cities. Today, Shanghai's per capita income is more than double other cities such as Mianyang and Suqian. To counter the potential for urban unrest, the federal government is starting a new plan for developing the regions to the north and west. In my ongoing research with Chinese coauthors, I have documented that this new regional favoritism will have carbon mitigation implications, because the northern cities such as Mudanjiangg, Jilin, and Tongliao are using significant amounts of coal for home heating and generating electricity.[19] As these cities grow, China's per capita carbon emissions will grow by more than if other urban areas grew. The northern cities are colder, and their power is produced using dirty coal-fired power plants. Thus, economic development in these cities will raise China's per capita urban emissions. But although northern inland urban growth poses carbon mitigation challenges, the households in these cities will face less climate adaptation risk. Such cities will enjoy climate amenity gains from living in a winter climate that is becoming warmer, and they face little flood risk.

## Vampire Cities

Around the world, capital cities receive special treatment. Beijing is no exception.[20] In recent years Beijing has been suffering from drought. Most economists would recommend demand-side responses such as raising local water prices, but the government has been investing in engineering solutions to divert water from nearby areas. Beijing started an "emergency" diversion program, pumping water from reservoirs in Hebei Province through a 305-kilometer canal to reservoirs within the city's jurisdiction. The canal is part of the much bigger South-North water diversion project, which aims to take even more water to Beijing from the Yangtze River in the south starting in 2014. The *China Daily News* reported at the end of January that US$3.11 billion would be invested in the project in 2010.[21]

The Chinese state's ability to divert water to Beijing distinguishes it from the United States, where nearby states such as Georgia and Florida sue each other over water rights to regional rivers. The judicial system and lawsuit settlements determine who has property rights to these scarce resources. Similar to the Los Angeles case discussed in chapter 4, the people of Beijing are not being given the right incentive to economize on water consumption. For political reasons, they are paying too low a price and thus are consuming too much water.

## Will Communist Party Mayors "Climate-Proof" Their Cities?

The Soviet Union severely degraded its environment as it focused on production and military development. If

China's Communist Party leaders follow a similar strategy, then it is highly unlikely that its politicians will take costly steps to adapt to climate change. But due to the incentives and performance criteria built into the system, politicians are likely to be rewarded for taking climate change seriously.

The central government evaluates the effectiveness of local government officials based on per capita income growth and reports of public unrest. Such performance criteria encourage local efforts to adapt to environmental challenges. If climate change is expected to disrupt a city's economy, either through shifting the climate amenity and repelling the skilled toward more pleasant cities or through direct productivity effects (the summer is too hot), then the mayor has a direct incentive of self-interest to become involved in adaptation measures.

Local government's prime source of revenue is from leasing land to developers.[22] All over the world, economists have documented that land prices and housing prices are higher in high-quality-of-life cities that offer economic opportunity. If the government can charge more per acre of land in cities that are perceived as "better," the local government faces the right incentives to build "great cities."

Local government leaders will have the right incentives to "climate-proof" the city if local land prices reflect both day-to-day quality of life and the expected cost of very low probability events like massive coastal floods. If the local populace believes that these events have no chance of taking place, then the "true" risk will not be reflected in local prices. Urbanites cannot respond to risks that they are not aware of.

There are three relevant cases here. In scenario 1, the public is aware that Shanghai is at risk due to climate change, and the politicians do nothing. In this case, local land prices fall. In scenario 2, the public is again aware, and the local mayor is proactive in protecting the city. In this case, land prices do not fall much if the people trust the mayor's competence. In scenario 3, the public is not aware of the climate change risk, and land price dynamics provide the mayor with no incentive to take costly action to protect the city. An open question in modern economics focuses on whether actuarial risk assessment (the truth in a hotter world) can deviate from the subjective perception of risk (what the typical person in Shanghai views as the risk of a major flood). Although economists have assumed "rational expectations" (that perception and reality are the same) for years, climate change may pose a sharp test of this assumption. Urbanites will have an easier time adapting to climate change if we have "rational expectations" and update our beliefs over time as climate scientists learn more about climate change.

Fear of local protest represents another means for encouraging adaptation efforts. A mayor's probability of losing his or her job increases if the people are protesting. The urban poor are most likely to participate in riots. Richer households have the resources to take care of themselves. In China today, the urban poor mainly consist of a huge number of floating laborers who migrate to booming cities in their search for jobs and income. Within these cities, they tend to live in squatter areas that are often not under state control. Because these communities are located within the city's broader geographical area but are not part of the city's political jurisdiction, an awkward incentives issue arises. The local political leaders have no incentive to protect such squatter areas. Climate change could sharply injure quality of life in such areas, but the state would have little incentive to provide electricity or flood relief to protect such areas.

## My Bet

While environmentalists and economists continue to debate the vague question of whether "economic growth is good for the environment," China's recent experience highlights that growth is good for adapting to climate change. China will soon resemble the United States in having a large number of mega-cities located in various geographical areas, which will provide diverse households with a menu of locational possibilities. Chinese skilled households will vote with their feet—as those of us in the United States already do—and locate in desirable, high-quality-of-life cities. Recognizing this mobility will provide strong incentives for urban politicians to protect quality of life and enact policies that help cities cope with climate change.

I must admit that I can't figure out how proactively China is pursuing "climate-proofing" for its major coastal cities such as Shanghai and Hong Kong. China clearly wants these cities to continue to thrive. Similar to the case of Manhattan, any "doom and gloomers" who hint that these coastal cities face major sea level rise challenges may raise issues that Shanghai's boosters would prefer be downplayed. During my trip to Beijing, I was surprised by the seeming unwillingness to discuss whether Shanghai faces "serious challenges" from future sea level rise. One professor expressed some concern that I be careful about what I said in my public lectures. I interpreted this as a hint that "if a fancy UCLA professor states that Shanghai flooding may be a future risk, this could create trouble as the media pick up the story and run with it." I did not intend to cause a scene. I merely wanted to take the temperature of some of the leading environmental policy scholars at their universities to get a better sense of whether China's academics were engaging in the scenario planning that Mayor Bloomberg's team in New York is doing and that San Diego has done with its 2050 report (discussed in chapter 3). In my research, I have not been able to find detailed documents assessing how climate change will affect Hong Kong and Shanghai equal to the quality of the reports that have been produced for New York City (see chapter 5) or San Diego (see chapter 3). That said, I admit that I do not speak Chinese, and Google's capacity to help me search the world may be limited.

Relative to other developing countries, China has an adaptation edge in terms of its population's skills and its governance. As we will see in the next chapter, climate change in the developing world will raise the risk of civil war, urban disease epidemics, and mass death from natural disasters. Due to its recent economic development, China will be spared such horrible outcomes.

# 7

# BONO'S ANXIETY

Risk is nothing new in the developing world. Consider vehicle accidents. The World Health Organization reports that 1.2 million people died from road traffic injuries in 2002; 90 percent of these deaths took place in low- and middle-income countries.[1] Ethiopian car drivers face a risk of death eighty times higher than drivers in Japan.[2] In these poor nations, the old transport modes of walking, bike riding, and motorcycles jostle for scarce road space with the booming number of cars. New drivers are not yet driving as well as Mario Andretti, and the cops are often not enforcing basic traffic laws. Climate change will amplify risk in the developing world because urbanites there will face extra risks from flooding, heat waves, and high air pollution levels.

Unlike richer nations, developing nations will have to cope with two key challenges. First, although those living in the developing world are well aware that they face high risk from natural disasters every day, they lack the facilities and institutions necessary to deal with it well. The urban poor face the greatest risks from climate change—induced events such as heat waves and flooding. Relative to richer households, they have less access to medical services and the kinds of goods that can offset climate exposure (like air conditioning and refrigeration). Within a city, high-quality land is more expensive than marginal land (for instance, land in flood zones), so the poor choose to live in the lowest-quality, least desirable parts of the city, where rents are low, but they face the greatest risk from natural disasters. This is really no different than the choices that the poor face in, say, Los Angeles, where Barbra Streisand lives in the serenity of Malibu and poorer households live in the hotter, more polluted East LA.

Second, billions of people still live in rural areas in the developing world. It is unknown how farmers in such nations will cope in a hotter world. But it's clear that a hotter future means an increase in the urban poor.

### Farming Adaptation

In developing nations, the majority of people still live in rural areas. Over time, millions will move to the cities seeking better opportunities. This migration will accelerate if climate change reduces the income that rural people earn from farming. Farmers seeking to increase their household income will compare what they are earning with their best guess about what they could earn living and working in a city. Farmers will be more likely to move to the cities as the gap between urban and rural income grows.

Agricultural economists continue to study how farmers in various nations respond to changing climate conditions. If such farmers cannot easily adapt to changes in rain patterns and winter and summer temperatures, climate change could sharply reduce their production and hence their income. One recent Massachusetts Institute of Technology study estimated that in India by the year 2070, climate change could reduce agricultural output by 25 percent if farmers continue to use their current production methods.[3]

Farmers differ with respect to the quality of their land, their knowledge about growing different crops, and their access to capital markets for financing large up-front investments that would allow them to switch crops. For example, growing some crops may require a tractor or active irrigation. These investments can cost a significant amount of money; small farmers may be less able to afford this and thus will suffer more during a time of climate change. Smarter, nimbler farmers endowed with high-quality land and having access to savings will be most able to adapt and remain profitable in our hotter world. But many of today's farmers do not fit this description.

Such suffering farmers may resort to violence. More than two-thirds of the countries in sub-Saharan Africa have experienced civil conflict in which millions have been killed since 1960. One recent research project documented that the probability of civil war in this region rises when the average temperature is higher.[4] A 1-degree Celsius increase in average temperature raises the risk of civil war by a whopping 49 percent! Under the assumption that the relationship between annual temperature and the probability of civil war is stable over time, the researchers use climate change models for this African region and predict that by the year 2030 there will be 393,000 deaths caused by climate change. Given the importance of climate for farm productivity relative to urban productivity, much of the disruption caused by temperature changes must take place in rural regions. Even in cities, violence can be affected by climate conditions. Research in the United States examining urban riots in the 1960s has documented "climate coincidences" that heavy rainfall in cities lowered the probability of such riots.[5]

For violence to erupt, many farmers must not have access to other coping strategies. Like Mel Gibson's foes in the *Mad Max* movies, people are fighting to the death over scarce natural resources. In *Mad Max*, the scarce commodity was gasoline; in Africa the fight would be over food and water. Economists continue to debate the effectiveness of foreign aid in alleviating these problems.[6] Encouraging migration to cities could be one means of defusing tension among desperate people.

Social scientists have studied how farmers cope with climate conditions. The World Bank has surveyed thousands of small farmers in many developing countries and collected detailed information about what agricultural products they grow and what climate conditions they face. The ideal "experiment" would take one farmer and study how his or her choices about crops and production techniques change in a broad range of climates (e.g., places that are hotter, have less rainfall, and have less access to irrigation). This would yield very useful information for predicting how farmers will change their behavior as climate change takes place. Of course this experiment cannot be conducted, but the World Bank tries to approximate it by identifying similar farmers (same age, ethnicity) who live in different climate zones. A comparison of the choices they make is useful for understanding how poor farmers cope with climate conditions. World Bank research that focused on Sri Lankan farmers highlights the importance of rainfall for farm output. This indicates that what climate change does to the monsoons may be more important than its temperature impacts.[7]

Many studies have focused on China's farmers. China continues to have a large rural population. Today, it ranks first in worldwide farm output, primarily producing rice, wheat, potatoes, sorghum, peanuts, tea, millet, barley, cotton, oilseed, and pork. Recent World Bank research has examined how Chinese farmers have responded to past climate variation to test whether they are nimble in changing their behavior in the face of climate variability. This research concludes that Chinese farmers adapt to climate changes by shifting to irrigation (where possible) and switching crops. With warmer temperatures, they are more likely to increase irrigation and grow oil crops, wheat, and especially cotton.[8]

While climate scientists today continue to debate what is the best model for forecasting future rainfall and temperature conditions, farmers will live through these conditions in the near future. Such farmers will recognize that their survival hinges on understanding the changing rainfall patterns. A naïve farmer will simply extrapolate about next year's rainfall based on the previous couple of years. A more sophisticated farmer will recognize that there is fundamental uncertainty about the changing climate and will be eager to talk to NGOs and other trusted sources of information based on formal climate modeling.

## The Growth of the Urban Poor

Environmental refugees are people who migrate due to changing environmental conditions in their origin nation.[9] Farmers who move to the cities because of climate change can be thought of as "climate change refugees." Given their initially low level of income, such migrants are likely to live in informal slum housing. The 2003 United Nations *Global Report on Human Settlements* estimates that 924 million people, or 31.6 percent of the world's urban population, lived in slums in 2001. In cities where a fixed amount of land is occupied by slum housing, the urban density will rise. If local governments do not have the revenue or the desire to provide basic services such as clean water and sanitation for a growing urban population, climate change–induced environmental refugees can unintentionally trigger local urban quality-of-life challenges. Risk of contagious disease in these communities will rise. Housing costs will rise as newcomers compete for scarce housing against the incumbents, and wages will decline as newcomers bid down local wages.

Urbanites could face higher food prices if local agriculture suffers from climate shocks. This outcome is especially likely if the nation does not actively participate in international trade.

Some nations erect high trade barriers such as tariffs and quotas to protect domestic producers. Mean agricultural tariffs are more than 100 percent in South Asia and the non-EU countries of Western Europe (104 percent). In Africa, average tariffs for the sub-Saharan and northern regions range from 71 to 75 percent.[10] Suppose that Ethiopian consumers purchase $100 worth of food in the United States. They would pay an extra $72 to import it into their home country. This border tax means that domestic consumers pay high prices for international imports. Without easy access to international imports, such urban consumers are at risk of being "price gouged" by domestic farming interests.

There have been recent projections that wheat production in major developing nations such as India and China may decline dramatically due to climate change.[11] The open question is how this supply shock will affect urban food prices in the medium-term future. If these nations participate in global trade, urban consumers seeking basic food staples can import products from other nations whose agricultural output has suffered less from climate change. In this sense, globalization offers developing countries an implicit insurance policy against shocks that injure specific sectors of the economy, such as agriculture.

## Rising Inequality in Cities

Urban population growth does more than simply scale up the size of cities. Typically, it also creates a more diverse urban population. Diversity is a defining characteristic of major cities. Diverse cities offer a far greater range of jobs, cultural opportunities, and even cuisine. University presidents and urban economists celebrate the benefits of diversity. After all, we can only learn from people who differ from us. But diversity imposes costs, because such cities will feature an electorate that disagrees on policy priorities. If everyone in a city were identical, it would be easy for this homogenous population to agree on a climate change adaptation strategy involving taxes and government expenditure.

Recent social science research has documented an ugly fact. People are less altruistic in terms of time and money when they live in more diverse communities.[12] It is unknown whether income inequality or ethnic diversity is a more important predictor of "bad civic behavior," but this uncomfortable correlation remains clearly visible in the data. In thinking about adaptation to climate change, this matters because the elites in big cities in the developing world may be unwilling to support policies that implicitly redistribute income to the poor, who disproportionately suffer more of climate change's costs. Why are the wealthy so stingy? Aside from not caring about the victims, the elites may be worried that if they were generous in providing public goods, they would be "rewarded" for this by even more rural people moving to their city. In California, San Francisco and Santa Monica have experienced this firsthand with their generosity to the homeless.

Diverse cities have favored interest groups and outsiders. Around the world, politicians keep key prices low to keep the households in their territory happy. Consider the water pricing in Los Angeles discussed in chapter 4—or electricity pricing. In nations such as Venezuela, energy prices are kept very low. This benefits households that are connected to the grid, but it means that the utilities have no incentive to expand coverage, because they lose money on each new hookup. Therefore new migrants to its cities do not enjoy access to basic services that we take for granted and that are necessary for adapting to climate change.

If we were to interview the mayor of a city in a developing country, he or she would point out that many of the residents live illegally in informal residences. Because they are not formally recognized as city residents, they escape taxation, but they are also not provided with basic services. Richard Arnott, an urban economist, put it like this, "The limited fiscal capacity of developing country governments makes the provision of urban infrastructure, including transportation, water, electricity, solid waste disposal, sewage, fire and police protection, schools, and medical facilities, more difficult. In informal settlements, these problems are compounded by the government's poor knowledge of their current state and inability to control their future development."[13]

One method to empower the urban poor would be to give them formal property rights to their squatter land. This policy shift has long been supported by the Peruvian economist Hernando de Soto.[14] Recent empirical research conducted by Erica Field in Peru documents that households invest more in improving the quality of their homes when they are granted formal property rights to the dwelling. She finds that land titling is associated with a 68 percent increase in the rate of housing renovation within only four years of receiving a title.[15] Home renovations take many forms, but costly investment in sanitation and protecting the home against flood risk are examples of actions that are encouraged by formal land title that would help the family to adapt to climate change.

### The Public Health Challenges Caused by Urban Population Growth

Urbanization is taking place at a faster rate in the developing world than in rich nations.[16] This makes sense: the developed world is already well urbanized, so its rate of growth is bound to be slower. Climate change is likely to increase urban density in the poorest parts of cities in less developed countries (LDCs). This will bring with it the dangerous risk of contagion from infectious diseases such as cholera. Polluted urban water poses a great challenge to the public. People infected with cholera suffer acute diarrhea. Cholera is transmitted from person to person through ingestion of water contaminated with the cholera bacterium, usually from feces or other effluent. The source of the contamination is typically other cholera patients, when their untreated diarrhea discharge is allowed to get into waterways or into groundwater or drinking water supplies.[17]

Public health experts are also quite worried about an increase in malaria cases in the developing world. Increases in global average temperature increase malaria risk rates, and hundreds of millions of people could be infected. A disease outbreak on such a scale will overwhelm the capacity of poor cities to provide health care for them.

It may seem that malaria risk is directly related to living in a hot place, but geography is not a sufficient condition for explaining malaria risk. Thomas Schelling, the 2007 Nobel Laureate in economics, wrote:

Malaria is no problem in the United States, Canada, or Western Europe. Climate does not altogether explain the lack of malaria; malaria got its name in ancient Italy and was serious in the United States a century ago. It is now associated with the tropics. But consider Singapore and Malaysia, two nations separated by a kilometer of seawater. Their climates are identical. There is virtually no malaria in Singapore; malaria is serious in Malaysia. If anyone living in Singapore does get malaria (by spending a weekend in Malaysia) he or she is probably in good health to begin with and gets necessary medical care. Singapore of course has the advantage of being small and rich, so environmental measures can take care of any mosquitoes. But this is the point of the comparison: Singapore and Malaysia were identical not only in climate but in development forty years ago. Both have developed, but Singapore spectacularly. If Malaysia can reach, through a second forty years of development, where Singapore reached in its first forty years, it should no longer be at the mercy of the mosquito.[18]

If climate change increases the risk of urban disease, this can have serious consequences for poor households. Put simply, sick children do not learn much in school. Health and investing in human capital go hand in hand. If parents anticipate that a child's life expectancy will be short, there is little reason to invest time and money attending school. This sad calculus means that health and wealth go hand in hand. If climate change threatens public health in developing countries' cities, it could play a role in slowing down rising educational attainment and skill formation in these countries—both of which are essential for economic growth—and could prove to be very costly for long-term economic development.

## Deaths from Natural Disasters

In January 2010 Haiti suffered massive loss of life from an earthquake. In late February 2010 Chile experienced a much more severe earthquake, but it caused many fewer fatalities. In my past research, I have documented that earthquakes of the same intensity cause much more death in poor nations than in rich ones.[19]

Between 1990 and 2004, an average of 52,000 people died each year worldwide in natural disasters.[20] This death count is mostly centered in poor nations. In poor cities, people live in very high population densities. Unlike in richer nations, which have access to better transportation systems, millions of people are living close to places of work and shops so that they can walk, bike, or take a bus to them. Living at high density, in low-quality housing, and on land that has not been protected from potential disasters such as floods, places plenty of people at risk. In the poorest nations, economic development actually increases the death count from natural disasters because more people move to the cities, increasing urban population density.

In the case of deaths from floods, for nations whose GDP per capita is less than $5,600, economic development is associated with more deaths from floods. But for nations with incomes greater than $5,600, researchers have documented that further economic development is associated with declining death counts from flooding. This $5,600 threshold point is not a law of physics. It was estimated based on disaster death data covering ninety-five nations between 1975 and 2002.[21]

Climate change will cause more flooding, and cities in the developing world will be even more at risk. Some of this urban risk is due to geography. In many developing countries, the coastal cities are the richer ones because they actively participate in international trade. The sad irony here is that this draws more people to live in them rather than in a "safe" inland city.

Coastal cities obviously face more risk from sea level rise. A recent Organization for Economic Cooperation and Development study that investigated urban coastal flooding in 130 major cities highlights that poor cities are vastly overrepresented among cities at risk:

> Around half of the total population exposure to coastal flooding caused by storm surge and damage from high winds is contained in just ten cities today. Most of these cities are located in the developing world. Mumbai has the highest number of people exposed to coastal flooding. But by 2070, Kolkata (Calcutta) will be the most vulnerable, with the exposed population expected to increase over seven times to more than 14 million people. Over the coming decades, the unprecedented growth and development of the Asian mega-cities will be a key factor in driving the increase in coastal flood risk globally. In terms of population exposure, Kolkata is closely followed by Mumbai, Dhaka, Guangzhou, Ho Chi Minh City, Shanghai, Bangkok and Myanmar. Miami is in ninth place and would be the only top ten city in a currently developed country, while Hai Phong in Vietnam is ranked tenth.[22]

Urban damage caused by natural disasters can be reduced through defensive investments. Unfortunately, many cities in the developing world have not planned ahead for anticipated natural disasters. Consider Calcutta's flooding challenge. This city has suffered from a failure to keep its canal system operating. For centuries the canals provided drainage, but the Calcutta Municipal Corporation admits that choked canals have been a major cause of the prolonged periods of being waterlogged.[23] Past attempts to clear the canals have come up against hundreds of thousands of encroachers—squatters—on the banks. Engineers in charge of making the canals function have submitted proposals to revive the canals, but they would require evicting the squatters.[24] Politicians in Calcutta will face the problem of fighting an incumbent group who must feel that they have de facto property rights to the canals (as their home), in the name of protecting the greater population through properly functioning canals.

Similar problems arise in West Africa's mega-cities. With a total population of around 10 million, Lagos has made inadequate provisions for basic infrastructure to cope with flooding. "'Normal' rainfall brings flooding to many areas of the city, largely as a result of the inadequacies in provision for sewers, drains and wastewater management. The lack of solid-waste collection compounds the problem as wastes block gutters and drains. In addition, many buildings have been erected in ways that block storm-water routes. Little attention is given to clearing the drains, in advance of periods of the year when rain is expected."[25]

In both Calcutta and Lagos, local government is not providing the basic services that people take for granted in U.S. cities. Why is government not up to the job?

## Government to the Rescue?

I n a fantasy democracy, benevolent, omniscient government officials would anticipate the needs and desires of their constituents. The government would collect taxes to provide the basic services such as clean water, street safety, and roads that the public needs to have a properly functioning, equitable city. In the real world, politicians are motivated by their own self-interest in being reelected and potentially becoming rich and powerful. Some politicians will be committed to improving the lives of the less fortunate, but others will seek to enrich themselves, their families, and their friends. Some politicians may be beholden to special interests that have made generous campaign contributions.

Aware that the public is not able to monitor their activities, these politicians have ample discretion to pursue their own goals. The absence of competitive elections and watchdog independent media (e.g., the *New York Times* and muckraker television shows such as *60 Minutes*) means that elected officials will not be held accountable for not serving the public's interest. However, there are countervailing forces at work. Educational attainment is increasing in the developing world, and literate people will invest more of their time in following the news. This demand for information will create a market for news sources that will investigate how politicians are performing.

One recent economics study examined Indian states between 1958 and 1992 to study how politicians respond to food production shocks. The authors documented that in the states where a larger percentage of people read newspapers, the government was much more proactive in providing basic services in the face of a bad food shock.[26] Literacy allows the voters to cheaply monitor politicians' efforts on their behalf. In Indian states where literacy is low, politicians are aware that they are less likely to be held accountable for not responding to crises. This suggests that climate change will increase inequality across Indian states, because more educated areas will fare better as their politicians work for the people, unlike those in poorer, more backward regions.

Corruption is a crucial determinant of whether a city will be able to cope with climate change. Quantitative measures of corruption indicate that poor nations suffer from more corruption. Corruption degrades the quality of government services, in part because of how it affects a government's public finances. Less revenue is collected that can be spent on public services, because it is diverted to the pockets of leaders and cronies. With public funds skimmed off, government has fewer resources to spend on necessary urban infrastructure. In more corrupt nations, the government spends too much money per unit of services delivered because public contracts to build canals or sewage systems are given to friends of the government (who then pay kickbacks) rather than holding an arm's-length auction and giving the procurement contract to the lowest bidder. The net result of this system is that friends of the government benefit, but basic services are not provided, and when the inevitable floods and other shocks occur, there is great suffering.

## Economic Development and Carbon Emissions

When ranking nations and cities with respect to their overall "greenness," developing countries score well on at least one criterion. Because they are poor, they are not producing much greenhouse gas emissions. "Green City" and "Green Nation" rankings that place a relatively high weight on greenhouse gas contributions actually rank LDC nations and cities higher. It is ironic that cities and nations that do not contribute much to causing climate change will bear most of its brunt.

Today, economic development continues to translate into more greenhouse gas emissions. In the absence of explicit carbon pricing, economic development is associated with households consuming more fossil fuels and electric utilities using fossil fuels. We can expect that all over the world urbanites in developing nations will embrace parts of the "American Dream," demanding their own private transportation, larger homes, personal electronics, and other electric appliances that we love so much.

There are some countervailing forces at work. As nations grow richer, households have fewer children. Consider Vietnam. In 1980, a randomly selected woman in the fifteen to forty-nine age group had on average 5.9 children; by 2000 this number had shrunk to 2.3, and it is expected to shrink to 1.85 by 2050.[27]

Urbanization slows national population growth through changing fertility patterns. This can offset some of the greenhouse gas produced by the urban productivity effect. Women have numerous employment opportunities in cities. There are a growing number of two-career households all over the world. Urban employment opportunities encourage women to marry later and delay having their first child. Anticipating that they will live in an urban area with labor market opportunities gives school-aged women a greater incentive to invest in their human capital. Given that cities raise women's wages and offer a thick local labor market, women have greater opportunities outside the home in cities. This raises the cost of having children and encourages urban households to choose "quality" over "quantity." Urban land is more expensive than rural land, which also provides an incentive for smaller households. In cities such as Beijing, households are spending a large share of their income on housing, and extra space is quite expensive.

The developing world has another potential advantage. One benefit of developing later in time is that a nation can "leapfrog" and embrace the best technology in the world, avoiding many of the "mistakes" that the developed nations have made. Just because the United States has built many coal-fired power plants does not mean that developing countries that are now building more power plants have to follow our lead. Given the long life of durables such as highway infrastructure, buildings, and power plants, we have to live with decisions we made decades ago in the United States to erect buildings that are highly energy inefficient; to create a transportation network that revolves around private, gasoline-powered vehicles; and to live spread out at a low population density.

In the developing world, nations do not need to follow our high-carbon path. Consider the example of telephone communication. In the United States, billions of dollars have been spent on underground cables, but in Africa such investments have been bypassed in favor of cell phone towers. A key issue that will arise in the near future is sharing best technology among nations. The carbon impact of LDC economic development will be much lower if the rich nations share their intellectual property (such as blueprints for renewable power generation) with developing nations.

Just as in the developed world, LDCs face a fundamental tension between mitigation and adaptation. As billions of households in developing cities grow richer, they will demand consumer durables such as cars and air conditioners, which we take for granted. The sheer aggregate growth in consumption and electric power generation will scale up the world's greenhouse gas emissions.

Access to clean technology is crucial for breaking this link between economic development and greenhouse gas production. Billions of people in the developing world do not have access to basic electricity. This exposes them to much higher smoke particulate levels as they use dirty fuels such as wood and dung for heating and cooking. The United Nations has estimated that it will cost over $600 billion to help developing countries build power plants using renewables, relative to the cost of building power plants using conventional dirty fuel sources such as coal.[28] This raises an interesting redistribution issue of who will pay for this "green push" in the developing world. The win-win would be if the developed countries were willing to pay this bill. Taxpayers in such nations as England might convince themselves that this transfer offers a "win-win" of giving resources to LDC countries that their people want and mitigating the carbon challenge.

## Economic Development Will Facilitate Adaptation

The urban poor do not have the resources to protect themselves, and their nations' federal and local governments are often unable or unwilling to devote the financial resources to protect them. Faced with this reality, their best coping strategy is to grow richer so that they can protect themselves.

Climate change makes it more difficult for poor nations to develop. An ongoing debate in economics has focused on the deep question of why poor countries are poor. Similar to a Bud Light commercial in which dudes argue if the beer "tastes great" or is "less filling," some economists yell that the answer is "bad geography" (e.g., the country is landlocked or too close to the equator and too hot), while others counter that the villain is "bad institutions" (i.e., corruption and lack of protection of property rights, objective media, and rule of law). Unfortunately, we cannot run an experiment in which we randomly move a well-functioning economy close to the equator and see if it falls apart, or take a dictatorship, install the U.S. Constitution, and hand out copies of the *New York Times*. We are forced to rely on certain "natural experiments," such as the divergent paths between East Germany and West Germany during the communist years or between North and South Korea since World War II. In both cases, we see the geographical "twins" diverge big time. These cases highlight the likely importance of institutions. But leading economists such as Jeff Sachs have noted the high rates of malaria and low productivity in nations close to the equator and have argued that geography plays a key role in long-term economic development.

A recent intriguing study sheds new light on the role of geography in determining economic performance. Melissa Dell, Benjamin Jones, and Benjamin Olken argue, based on fifty years' worth of data for nations around the world, that heat waves have made poor nations poorer. Their bottom line is that poor nations, not rich nations, suffer income loss from temperature extremes. They estimate that in poor countries a 1-degree C temperature increase in a given year reduced economic growth in that year by about 1.1 percent. On the other hand, since World War II the U.S. economy has grown by about 3 percent per year. By the law of compound interest, a nation that grows at 3 percent per year enjoys a doubling of per capita income in twenty-four years, while a nation that grows at 2 percent per year enjoys a doubling of per capita income in thirty-six years. This suggests that for poor nations, the effect of temperature is huge, and if this relationship continues to hold into the future, it portends scary consequences from climate change.

Dell, Jones, and Olken believe that declines in agricultural output during hot years are only part of the reason temperature changes have such huge effects on poor nations. They document that urban productivity also declines during hot years. In poor countries, there are fewer scientific publications issued in hot years, which suggests that higher temperatures may impede innovative activity. Higher temperatures also lead to political instability in poor countries, as shown by distinctive patterns in changes in national leaders.[29]

Richer people have the resources to protect themselves from many of the risks that climate change will pose. They live in housing located in relatively safer places and built of higher-quality materials that can withstand floods and hurricanes. With growth, a city's medical services improve to treat diseases such as malaria.

Climate change raises the risk that cities face. Richer people are willing to pay to avoid such risk. After all, we would never expect to see Donald Trump working as a construction worker. He pays other people to put up a building for him. To "climate-proof" cities requires making up-front expenditures now. The benefits of such investments hinge on how much urban residents value avoiding risk. Economists have documented that as nations get richer, their citizens reveal a taste for safety. Using data from the United States, India, and Taiwan on the wage premium for working in risky jobs such as construction and mining, independent teams of economists have shown that larger "combat pay" is offered (measured in higher wages) for working in such jobs as the nation gets richer.[30] Economic development provides cities with the capital to invest in adaptation strategies and increases household demand for such protection.

Economic growth and educational attainment go hand in hand. A richer nation can invest more in great universities (think of the Ivy League), and these great universities produce the next generation of innovators who help to enrich a nation (think of the Google/Stanford nexus). Chapter 3 discussed the many environmental benefits associated with highly educated cities. I recognize that this optimism hinges on the assumption that the educated and wealthy will not wall themselves off from everyone else in the city. If the elite are able to form a moat around their own safe areas, their activism to protect their communities will offer no benefits for the city's populace as a whole.

As educational attainment rises in the developing world, people will improve as problem solvers, a useful skill in our hotter world. Evidence from Finland supports this optimistic claim. In the Finnish army, due to compulsory service, all males take an intelligence test at age nineteen or twenty. A team of economists accessed individual test results from all exams between 1982 and 2001. They tied these IQ test results to the Finnish Central Securities Depository Registry (which has records on all Finnish households' portfolios and trades). This bizarre but brilliant data merge allowed them to study the effect of IQ on stock market participation and portfolio holdings. People with higher IQs are more likely to participate in the stock market and buy stocks. Low IQ correlates with a more poorly diversified portfolio.[31] This means that low cognitive people are not protecting themselves from risk that they could avoid. A poorly diversified portfolio means that the low-IQ people in Finland are putting "all of their eggs in one basket."

I do not view IQ as an immutable trait. In recent years, social scientists have strongly dismissed the social determinism implicit in Charles Murray's *The Bell Curve*. Nobel Laureate James Heckman has convincingly argued that "learning begets learning, skill begets skill."[32] Intuitively, skill formation and human development are an outcome of an ongoing, dynamic process. As we invest our time in improving our ability to solve problems, we will become more agile at coping with climate change. We know that climate change will expose us to situations we cannot even imagine today, but the Finish research indicates that the "problem solvers" among us will have an advantage in coping in this new world.[33] Nobody should start thinking about Huxley's *Brave New World*. This is not a zero-sum game. "Beta people" such as Homer Simpson can become "alpha people" through investing in their own skill formation.

## History Lessons on the Benefits of Growth

Economic history provides several lessons about how improvements in our standard of living have helped us fend off disease and quality-of-life risk in the past. These same lessons are relevant for predicting quality-of-life trends in future LDC cities facing climate change.

Economic historians have emphasized that changes in diet over time, associated with a rising standard of living, such as eating more meat and other protein, have protected the population from disease. A healthier, well-fed population can withstand illness, heat waves, and cold waves with fewer health consequences.

Historians of public health in cities have documented that U.S. cities made great progress in investing in water treatment and sewage infrastructure between 1880 and 1940. In 1880 U.S. cities were deadly compared to the countryside. A white man living in a U.S. city in 1880 had a life expectancy ten years shorter than if he lived in a rural area. By 1940 this urban "death premium" had vanished as major cities invested large sums in water treatment and garbage collection. Between 1880 and 1940 U.S. cities were developing, which allowed them to build large sanitation systems; consequently they enjoyed sharp reductions in death from waterborne diseases such as typhoid.[34]

What triggered these major public investments continues to be debated. One possibility focuses on risk mitigation. Fear of contagion from cholera, typhoid, and other infectious diseases increased, and this fear of epidemic triggered investment. An alternative view is that innovations in financial markets, in particular the ability to issue municipal bonds, allowed major cities to finance the large up-front expenditures required for big engineering projects. These bond issues offered buyers the opportunity to receive a fixed interest rate on their investment. By issuing these IOUs, cities were able to borrow a large amount of money to pay for the big engineering projects.[35]

This same issue arises today in the developing world. Over the next one hundred years, developing nations will be building huge amounts of new infrastructure and even whole new cities to house the new urbanites. From a climate change adaptation perspective, I hope that these investments are sited in low-risk areas. Given that many major cities are located along the coasts and major rivers, the urbanizing population faces significant risk.

Upgrading buildings, bridges, roads, water treatment plants, and antiflood infrastructure in coastal areas will require larger up-front expenditure for construction materials. The benefits from such expenditures will accrue in future years, especially as climate change's shocks grow more severe. Although richer cities can afford such investments, cities in the developing world are unlikely to be able to finance capital improvements that require large up-front investments. To borrow our ugly economics jargon, such cities are "liquidity constraints"; they cannot use future profits and earnings as collateral and borrow today to finance worthy investments.

Ideally, international capital markets will provide LDC cities with the access to capital to underwrite expensive public investments in infrastructure such as sewage systems and the "smart" electricity grid that can protect the public from climate change. Infrastructure projects can cost billions of dollars up front, but they live on for fifty to one hundred years. Most developing nations do not have the resources to finance such investments, but Wall Street is always looking for investment projects offering a high rate of return. Access to international capital markets will offer mutually beneficial trades between LDC cities and Wall Street. The net result of such investments will be safer cities.

## Where Not to Buy Real Estate in the Developing World

Taking a long-term perspective, the cities in the developing world that face the largest problems caused by climate change will be those that in the year 2070 are still poor, located on the coast, located near the equator, and led by corrupt governments. I must admit that I am not one of the great macro-economists. The year 2070 is sixty years from now. Think back to sixty years ago, in 1950. Economists viewed themselves as quite smart back then, but I doubt that many (any) predicted the economic growth of China, Japan, South Korea, or Taiwan. So I am not that confident in my ability to "name names" of who will and won't develop over the next sixty years.

Given these caveats, I am willing to name some cities that I would not advise buying property in: Dhaka, Jakarta, Manila, and Calcutta. Each sits close to the sea, is regularly hit with natural disasters, and is already quite hot. World environmental organizations regularly publish reports ranking them as the leading at-risk cities.[36] These cities are precariously located in coastal at-risk areas. Their population density is high. It is already hot in each of these cities, and at least up to this point, their governments do not appear to be up to the job of protecting them. I confess that I have never visited any of these cities, but their geography, institutions, and socioeconomic attributes all suggest that they are risky.

This has been a somber chapter. I recognize that climate change poses real threats to the people in developing countries. But the twentieth-century examples of Japan and South Korea and the twenty-first-century example of China highlight that economic development can quickly transform a nation. What is difficult to predict is how much of the coming adaptation effort in developing countries will be individuals protecting themselves through investments such as living in a safer location or purchasing higher-quality medicines and market products (e.g., air conditioners), and how much will be the state providing useful public goods (e.g., sea walls).

Every shock creates challenges and opportunities. I now turn to the opportunities created by climate change for various cities around the world.

# 8

# SEIZE THE DAY: OPPORTUNITIES FROM OUR HOTTER FUTURE

In the 1978 *Superman* movie—the first one starring Christopher Reeves—Lex Luthor, played by a smarmily evil Gene Hackman, unleashed a brilliant plan that would have made him rich had Superman not stepped in. Luthor purchased a large amount of western land far from the California coast, which he anticipated would become extraordinarily valuable—once he destroyed California with a man-made earthquake. Luthor's logic foreshadows an unappreciated fact: climate change will cause some cities and industries to boom.

Today we could buy one hundred homes in Detroit for the cost of one typical home near UCLA. Sell one home and buy one hundred other homes; that sounds like a profit of 99 homes! But there is of course no free lunch. The fact that West Los Angeles real estate is valued at one hundred times the value of Detroit real estate tells us something about quality of life and economic opportunities in both cities. But climate change could help Detroit make a comeback. If we believe that, maybe we should consider buying Detroit land now, before this news becomes common knowledge. The double punch of climate change and serious climate change mitigation efforts will help jump-start some of the older, colder Northeast and Midwest cities. The "New Detroit" of 2050 will have a warmer winter and be at relatively little risk of flooding.

Declining cities like Buffalo, Cleveland, and Detroit have tried many different strategies for stimulating growth. A partial list ranges from building downtown sports stadiums and arts centers to constructing expensive rail transit systems. On net, these well-meaning investments have not reversed the decline, and these cities continue to stumble around searching for the right formula to recover their past glory. In the current competitive landscape, that's unlikely.

It's easy to be skeptical about these cities' revival. But there are cities that are vibrant today—Boston and New York City, for instance—that languished back in the 1970s. When the Bronx was burning back in the 1970s, few there would have anticipated the gentrification and quality-of-life improvements that have taken place since the early 1990s. These revitalizations of cold-winter cities highlight that there is no reason to be fatalistic about the future of cities such as Detroit and Cleveland.

Climate change and the nation's brewing effort to combat it may provide the answer for these cities' economic recovery. As climate change rocks the status quo, it will create opportunities for new firms, new markets, and older cities to compete. Detroit's mayor can look for inspiration from Murmansk, Russia. The melting of the ice caps near the North Pole will create shorter shipping routes. According to the *New York Times*,

> Murmansk has a population of 325,000, making it the biggest city inside the Arctic Circle. The advantage of maritime shortcuts across the top of the world can be startling. For example, shipments from Murmansk to mid-continental North America by the well-worn route through the St. Lawrence Seaway and Great Lakes to Thunder Bay, in western Ontario, typically take 17 days. The voyage from Murmansk to Churchill is only 8 days under good conditions. . . . The same way an Arctic Bridge could drastically cut the distance to Canada, a revived Northern Sea Route could shorten the journey for goods and raw materials from Northeast Asia to Europe by 40 percent.[1]

All of Greenland is salivating at the opportunities that its melting ice will create. "The huge Greenland ice cap, some 3km (nearly 2 miles) deep in places, may threaten the rest of the world as it melts and so raises the sea level, but for locals it offers a bonanza: torrents of melt-water to spin turbines," wrote Adam Roberts.[2] "The government wants hydro to supply 80% or more of Greenland's power. Cheap and clean energy, plus a cool climate, could then lure investors. As Greenland's ice retreats, other economic activity will flourish. Miners are prospecting newly revealed rock for gold, rubies, diamonds and more. A bigger economic prize would be if long-promised deposits of oil and gas were found offshore. Disappearing sea ice is making that task easier."[3] There are many other cities that will see their lot improved in our hotter future.

## When the Weather Gets Better

Heat waves such as the 2006 heat wave in California (400 deaths), the 2005 heat wave in Arizona (100 deaths), and the particularly deadly heat wave in France in 2003 (14,800 deaths) garner the headlines, but cold waves may cause even greater mortality. To put it bluntly, cold waves kill.

In an interesting study, economists Olivier Deschenes and Enrico Moretti document that days with cold temperatures have a significant and long-lasting impact on mortality rates. The cumulative effect of one day of extreme cold during a thirty-day period is an increase in daily mortality by as much as 10 percent. Deschenes and Moretti find that across the United States, each cold day caused an extra 360 deaths. "We interpret this figure as a remarkably large number. For example, this total exceeds the annual deaths due to leukemia, homicide, and chronic liver disease cirrhosis. . . . Of course, there are sizable differences across cities in the incidence of cold related deaths. Minneapolis, Detroit, Cleveland, and Chicago are the most affected, with estimates ranging from 1.4% to 3.2% of annual deaths that could be delayed by changing the exposure to extreme cold days."[4]

Before climate change, households had to move from the Rust Belt to the Sun Belt to enjoy higher winter temperatures. For households that continue to live in Northeast and Midwest cities, climate change will offer this same health benefit of warmer winters without moving! Consider Pittsburgh: over the last thirty years its average February temperature has been 30.8 degrees F. One climate change model predicts that Pittsburgh County's average February temperature will be 36.2 degrees F by 2070. This 5.4-degree increase in average winter temperature will have a serious impact on reducing the mortality rate in Pittsburgh.

In contrast, consider Phoenix. Its historical February average temperature is 57.8 degrees F, and its July average temperature is 90.4 degrees F. The same climate model predicts that the average summer temperature will increase to 92.3 degrees F, whereas Pittsburgh's average August temperature is predicted to be 81.8 degrees F. In this comparison, climate change will cause Pittsburgh's climate to improve by more than Phoenix's. Phoenix is really hot in the summer and is predicted to get hotter as climate change kicks in. Whether these amenity dynamics will slow down or reverse the long-standing migration to the Sun Belt is unknown.

## Skiing

<sub></sub>

M any urbanites in cities like Buffalo and Cleveland will welcome warmer winters, but the ski industry will experience dramatic changes. Recall that snow melts at 32 degrees F. This crucial threshold point means that relatively warm ski areas in parts of Arizona, New Mexico, and the Lake Tahoe area in California and Nevada face the possibility of substantial reductions in the quality of snow and the risk of becoming wet mud piles. In this case, there will be sharp declines in home prices around those ski resorts. In contrast, some areas, such as high-altitude or northerly resorts in Colorado, Montana, and Wyoming, will see very little adverse impact of warming and perhaps will even see gains, as demand for their resorts increases from skiers coming to more northern locations.[5]

As ski opportunities decline in areas such as California but remain the same or improve in areas such as Montana, tourists will fly to these more northern locations. And when Montana wins, California will lose: one extra skier for Sun Valley is one fewer for Lake Tahoe. From the skiers' perspective, the loss (depending on where they live) is extra travel time. The big losers from climate change will be landowners in areas where the quality of skiing declines. The winners will be landowners in areas where ski demand will grow as climate change warms up (not too much) northern ski locations.

## International Trade

Globalization and trade in manufactured goods and agricultural products have played a key role in helping exporting nations such as China sharply reduce their poverty rate and improve the quality of life of consumers. Climate change will further increase the volume of such trading.

Think of an urban population that loves strawberries. The typical environmentalist might say, "To reduce our greenhouse gas emissions from transport, you should grow your own." But if climate change shifts the rain patterns, many cities will be located in regions that would not be able to grow their own strawberries. Cross-region trade guarantees that cities that cannot grow certain agricultural commodities can continue to enjoy consuming them by simply buying them from another region. In this sense, the ability to trade with many possible partners spanning the globe helps to protect urban consumers from a loss in diversity of their diet.

Trade in agricultural products is like shipping water from a wet region to a dry region (except that water is too heavy to ship). The wet regions can grow all sorts of fruits and vegetables; the dry regions can't. As long as drought regions have something of value that they can export back to the water-endowed regions in return for food, this trade will effectively allow those who live there to import water embedded in final output such as strawberries.

Trade across dispersed geographical areas gives us an adaptive advantage over other creatures. Ecologists are worried about how birds will continue to find food as their habitats are affected by climate change.[6] The survival of the fittest will be fought out in the animal world in a way that humans who trade will not face.

Yes, there is competition for jobs and homes, but much of this competition is mediated through markets. Where scarcities arise (e.g., food shortages), we will see local prices rise, and international food exporters will have an incentive to export to locations where the market price is higher.

Trade in agriculture is just the tip of the iceberg. For goods like a slice of pizza, there will not be a world market. If a pizza place in Moscow is offering you a slice for the ridiculously low price of two cents, you will not call it and place an order from Chicago. The transportation cost to ship it from Moscow to Chicago and its depreciation as you wait three days for the delivery would mean that two cents is still not a low enough price. But for many products, such as a new car or new computer, the shipping cost per value of the final product and the depreciation costs are quite low.

Some bemoan that Amazon.com has crushed local bookstores by offering a vast array of products at low prices. That company can ship its products anywhere, and people show little loyalty to the local bookstore as they seek out a good deal. Such international arbitrage—the principle of buy low, sell high—gives us protection that birds cannot enjoy. When birds are hungry in their old habitat, they must search for a new one. Our ability to import from multiple trading partners scattered around the world helps us to adapt to changing climate without having to seek a new habitat.

## The Intuition of Climate Change Adaptation
## Is the Absence of Arbitrage

---

Climate change's shocks and surprises will create many so-called arbitrage opportunities—the chance to profit because of imbalances in various markets. We'll be able to buy cheap and sell high—if we know where to look. Companies' self-interested pursuit of eager buyers will actually protect households in a climate-changed world. The Internet and smart phones provide people with an easy information flow that will keep them in the loop about good opportunities for both sellers and buyers.

The existence of these arbitragers means that our cities cannot run out of food because of climate change. Although such businesspeople cannot perfectly predict the weather and won't exactly know when droughts or heat waves will occur, they can make pretty good guesses. Suppose that they believe that Florida's orange crop will be horrible because of climate-related events. As orange prices rise around the United States, they will be ready to flood the market with substitutes such as lemons or apples, which consumers will seek out as they change their diet patterns and consume fewer oranges.

Los Angeles supermarkets cannot be barren after a bad California crop yield. The price of fresh fruits and veggies would rise, and this information would be spread around the world. Exporters in Mexico or elsewhere would become aware of this and would arrange to have their produce shipped to the LA stores; through this arbitrage the store's shelves would be restocked.

Trade and globalization protect us against localized shocks, but suppose that all agricultural growers around the world are likely to suffer the same shocks (e.g., drought). If all agricultural areas simultaneously experience the same bad shock, there will be no sellers of fresh fruit to cash in on the shortage. If agricultural producers anticipate that this global "doom" scenario can take place, they have an incentive to hold inventories. Just as Exxon can hold gasoline off the market and wait to sell next year at a higher price, food producers could follow a similar strategy. I recognize that fruit rots, but dried fruit has a life span of roughly one year. Although dried fruit is not exactly the same thing as fresh fruit, this would be one strategy to cope with nasty climate shocks. So I predict that climate change will lead to more dried fruit being produced. How much we suffer from climate change hinges on how well such dried fruit substitutes for fresh fruit in both taste and nutrients. Dried fruit has less Vitamin C, but it can be rich in other vitamins and dietary minerals.

## Innovation and Adaptation

In our hotter world, more than 7 billion people will be seeking new energy-efficient products for living comfortably under changing climate conditions. This will create new business opportunities. An entrepreneur who can develop an air conditioner that is effective at cooling but doesn't use much electricity can capture a huge world market and become very rich. The lure of this profit incentive creates a powerful desire for capitalists to focus their efforts on designing products that help people around the world cope with climate change. It is important to note that the entrepreneur's motivation is not altruism or charity. He or she seeks to become very rich. But the end justifies the means. Mother Teresa might not be impressed with the capitalists who seek to be the next Google, but the winning products (e.g., the next Toyota Prius) will sharply improve the world's quality of life in the face of climate change.

A defining feature of capitalism is the development of new products. The quality of market goods changes over time. Compare cars or airplanes in 1950 to those of today. Think of the personal computer in 1985 and today. Think of the range of medicines available today versus thirty years ago. Whether it is Diet Coke or cell phones, the Mac or Google Maps, capitalist firms continue to experiment. Such firms do not randomly try out new ideas. Instead, taking cues from rising prices, they focus their efforts on offering new products they believe they can make money selling. Put simply, capitalist firms evolve to cope with changing market circumstances.

The global market is crucial here. Suppose that China allows foreign firms to sell within the country. The potential to sell to 1.2 billion people with a growing share of middle-class and wealthy households provides an enormous incentive to design products that cater to this group. If consumers seek products that help them adapt, producers will have every incentive to deliver. New products are not cheap to develop.

Drug companies, for instance, emphasize that they spend billions on basic R&D to develop drugs and run their evaluation trials. The expectation that there is a large market to sell to provides the carrot for bearing this up-front risk. Globalization provides this market opportunity. In a world where domestic firms could only sell their output to domestic buyers, the market opportunities would be much smaller.

Over the course of the twentieth century, we expected that engineers could come up with solutions for pressing challenges, such as designing faster computers and better rockets for space exploration, even though the typical person doesn't understand how such discoveries work. An optimist would look at our recent track record in fields ranging from robotics, to military hardware, to computing and feel that our smart engineers will anticipate future headaches and cook up just-in-time solutions.

Technological optimists say that it's obviously true that necessity is the mother of invention, the world is filled with millions and soon billions of highly educated people, and these individuals are able to perceive and anticipate coming trends that they will further seek to capitalize upon. The first step to prevent doom is to diagnose that a problem is coming if we stick to the status quo—that there is, in fact, a necessity that will drive invention.

Just as Google has gotten rich by allowing people hungry for information to search the Internet efficiently, there will be future "green companies" that make a fortune selling mitigation and adaptation products. Their motive will be profit, but the end result will be a cheaper adaptation path.

Real-time information about our consumption patterns and the changing prices of scarce goods such as water and electricity will also push households to seek out efficient products (such as energy-efficient dishwashers). Today, there is much talk about the "smart grid." The basic ideas is that computer devices will be placed in our homes to provide us with hour-by-hour data about our electricity consumption. We could then temper our consumption to use the least possible electricity. Until recently, most households (including mine) were barely aware of our monthly electricity consumption, because the bills are not user friendly. Climate change will increase the demand for electricity, and climate change mitigation efforts (such as a carbon tax) will mean that we are increasingly generating our electricity using unreliable, renewable power generation (such as wind turbines). When the wind does not blow or the sun does not shine, these "green" renewables produce little power. Serious spikes in electricity prices are likely to occur. If households expect that they will face such high electricity prices on the hottest July days, they will have a strong incentive to seek out highly energy-efficient air conditioners. Conversely, if governments worry about "price gouging" and thus cap electricity prices, this would have a chilling effect on corporate investments in research and development of energy-efficient products. Ironically, to allow capitalism to help us adapt to climate change, the government must precommit to not protect "the victims."

Rising electricity prices will help to accelerate this green tech advance. Economists have documented the "coincidence" that car companies respond to rising gasoline prices by investing in research and development that allows them to offer much more fuel-efficient vehicles; in a similar fashion, makers of air conditioners respond to higher electricity prices by introducing new brands that are much more energy efficient. Rising energy prices signal scarcity to for-profit firms, and they respond by innovating in ways that economize on the scarce commodity (energy).[7]

## Risk Allocation Markets

As climate change introduces more risk into our day-to-day life, risk-averse households will seek out more insurance, giving the insurance industry a strong incentive to provide policies whose premiums differ by location. Unlike daredevils, the risk averse are willing to pay for certainty. They prefer $100 for sure rather than having a 50 percent chance of earning $250 and a 50 percent chance of earning $0.

Insurance plays a key role in day-to-day life. If your house burns down, if you are disabled, or if your spouse dies, these devastating events can cripple you emotionally and financially. An insurance contract cannot protect you against emotional pain, but the promise to make you whole again by giving you a large cash payout when you are at your low point helps you recover under stress. Millions of households reveal that they value the peace of mind when they purchase a range of insurance policies, including life, car, home, and disability.

Insurance companies have a tried-and-true formula for making money. Risk-averse households sign up for a policy that might say; "I promise to pay $4,000 a year as my premium. In return, if my home is destroyed then the insurance company will send me a $200,000 payment to help me rebuild or find a new home." The insurance company will make profits from this contract if the probability of a fire for your home in a given year is less than 2 percent. For example, suppose that one out of every one hundred homes burns down each year in a city. In this case, an insurance company that sells 300 insurance policies to people in the city would collect 300 × $4,000 = $1,200,000 in revenue. The actuarial best guess of the total set of policy holders whose homes would burn down would equal 3 (1/100 × 300), and the firm would pay out $600,000 in claims (3 × $200,000). Thus, this firm would earn a neat $600,000 in profits. If the insurance industry were competitive, firms would enter this industry until the premium price for a $200,000 policy equals $2,000 and profits would equal zero.

Climate change affects this arithmetic because it raises the probability that disaster will destroy any given home. After climate change the risk may be 4 percent rather than 2 percent per year. If the insurance company keeps the old rates, it will lose money. It would collect less in total premiums than it would have to pay out to victims in the new riskier world. As the company loses money, it will raise premiums and structure them to reward households that take actions to lower the probability that they will suffer a disaster.

Florida's insurance firms are already doing this, and it encourages homeowners to invest in precautions that lower their risk of home damage during a storm.

Climate change will increase demand for household and business insurance. For-profit insurers' policy pricing will send valuable signals about the relative risk of living in various areas. Put simply, insurance will be more costly to purchase in more risky (due to climate change) areas, pushing economic activity away from areas at risk from floods and fires to safer areas, and will reward homeowners and commercial building owners for taking proactive steps that minimize the probability of disaster when floods and fires do take place.

The fundamental challenge that insurance companies face is having enough money to cover their policies during bad times. Suppose that an insurance company sells a million insurance policies to homeowners in the state of Florida. If a massive hurricane hits Florida, all of these policy holders will suffer at the same time. Each will submit a claim to the insurance company demanding a payment. Clearly, the insurance company is holding a risky portfolio—one that climate change will make even more risky. The insurance company may be making big profits when things are calm, but when nasty storms take place, it could go broke. In the past, governments have had to step in and offer capital to insurance companies in times of trouble.

But today global financial innovation has helped to address this issue with the creation of catastrophe bonds, which allow insurance companies the opportunity to diversify their portfolios. An insurance company that has sold multiple home policies in a hurricane zone in Florida is at risk of losing a fortune if a major storm takes place. Anticipating this, the insurance company could sponsor a catastrophe bond, which would pass on the risk to investors. Investors would buy the bond, which might pay them some rate of return between 3 and 20 percent. If no hurricane hit Florida, the investors would make a healthy return on their investment. But if a hurricane were to hit Florida and trigger the catastrophe bond, then the principal initially paid by the investors would be used by the insurance company to pay its claims to policy-holders.[8] Innovation in financial markets protects risk-averse investors during a time of rising risk.

## New Insurance Opportunities versus Price Gouging

Climate change will create big profit opportunities for insurance companies that are nimble enough to accurately price the real-time risk that policy owners (such as homeowners) face in different locations. We will adapt more easily with better geographical risk models and a greater tolerance for extreme price discrimination.

One challenge for implementing such extreme price variation in insurance is our fundamental sense of fairness. Behavioral economists have documented that in day-to-day life, we have a strong preference for preserving the status quo and become angry when we feel we have been treated unfairly. In many laboratory experiments, economists have documented that undergraduate research subjects are willing to sacrifice a payment in order to punish another player in the game who has treated them unfairly.

Households that feel the insurance companies have engaged in price gouging will push their congressional representatives to protect them. The irony here is that to help us to adapt to climate change, we have to allow the insurance companies to "gouge" us. High insurance prices in at-risk areas (such as coastal properties) provide the right signal to households and firms to locate somewhere else. This signal helps to reduce the costs of climate change when sea level rise and flooding do take place in such zones.

We need to trust competition in this market. If the insurance companies were truly earning easy money by overcharging us, new competitors would enter the market (just as Toyota entered the car market when the American Big Three were dominating it) and sell cheaper insurance. This threat of competition rather than government regulation is the right way to discipline the insurance industry in the face of difficult-to-predict actuarial probabilities as climate change shifts the likelihood of future events.

Ideally, the insurance industry will be a constructive actor in helping us adapt to climate change. The industry has every incentive to be proactive in its climate impact modeling. It would be a disaster if this industry relied on retrospective, historical models in the face of climate change; insurers would lose a lot of money. A historical, statistical approach would ask the question, "Over the last fifty years, how many times has this geographical area flooded?" If the answer is three times over 10,000 days, then such a historical analysis would say that the probability of a flood on any subsequent day is 3/10,000 and would price the insurance policy accordingly. But in the face of climate change, using past natural disaster rates may sharply underestimate the likelihood of future events. In this case, the "art" of prediction and having a strong climate model become crucial inputs in predicting the likelihood of future events in a changing world.

The insurance industry is well aware that climate change poses new threats and opportunities for its business. London is a world capital of the insurance industry. Its boosters hope that thousands of new jobs will be created in the fast-moving industry. The insurance market is crucial for helping us adapt, but climate change could pose fundamental issues for the survival of this industry.

Climate change will shake up the status quo. Suppose that a company in a building close to a coast used to pay $2,000 per year for flood insurance. Now suppose that the insurer informs the company's owners that their premium will now cost $4,000 per year. What happens next? The company will be angry that its cost of doing business will rise sharply. It could threaten a lawsuit charging the insurance company with price gouging. On one level, there appears to be some merit in this charge. The price has jumped by 100 percent. But how will a jury respond when the insurance company puts climate modelers on the witness stand who testify under oath that their best models predict that the building in question is located in an area with objectively higher severe flood risk and that climate change is the cause of this increased risk? The insurance company would pounce on this claim and argue that the $4,000 per year price simply reflects the cost it must charge to barely make a profit in this new climate change–induced, riskier environment. If politicians choose to impose price ceilings on insurance contracts, the companies who purchase insurance will applaud at first, but then insurance companies will stop issuing policies, and the companies at risk from flooding will have no access to private insurance. In this case, in the face of climate change, a well-meaning government mandate to stop price gouging could actually cause insurance to dry up.

This would lead the companies in flood zones to take the gamble of not buying insurance, with the result that the government would be dragged in to play this role. Taxpayers would have a lot to grumble about as they watched their tax dollars being used to protect businesses and homes that chose to put themselves at risk.[9]

If governments prevent insurance companies from charging actuarially fair prices (i.e., those that reflect the underlying probabilities that accompany climate change), we will see these insurance firms refusing to issue policies in certain geographical areas. The government will then face a stark choice. If it sells insurance (presumably at a subsidized price), it must recognize that an unintended consequence of this is to encourage more households to live in a risky place. When the inevitable climate shocks occur, the government will have blood on its hands. Alternatively, the government could impose new zoning rules that move the victims away from at-risk areas. This paternalistic action would generate numerous lawsuits because property owners in the risky areas would view this as stealing their private property.

At the end of the day, the public wants a free lunch. We want to be offered our old low insurance, electricity, and water rates, and we want to be safe from climate change. In 1977 Meatloaf sang that "two out of three ain't bad." I can only offer you one out of two. The magic of the capitalist system is not Donald Trump's hair; instead, it comes from price signals. Only government has the power to muffle such signals. It should use such power sparingly and learn to trust the power of competition and individual choice. Climate change will create more business opportunities (and thus more solutions) if prices are allowed to float.

## Opportunities Created by Greenhouse Gas Emissions Reduction Efforts

In June 2009 the U.S. House of Representatives passed the American Clean Energy and Security Act, comprehensive legislation aimed at capping U.S. greenhouse gas emissions. The United States may soon develop a new nationwide market for greenhouse gas emissions. The lingering effects of the national recession have certainly dampened the Senate's willingness to tackle this issue, but President Obama's active role at the December 2009 Copenhagen Climate Conference strongly suggests that he will use some of his political capital to pursue reducing our nation's greenhouse gas production. While economists hypnotize the general public with our endless discussions of the relative merits of carbon taxes versus introducing a pollution permit market (also known as cap and trade), at the end of the day both of these policies would create strong incentives to reduce our economy's greenhouse gas emissions. If we follow Europe and enact regulation of this sort, this will create new opportunities for our economy.

At the same time that the federal government is taking steps to reduce our economy's carbon emissions, some liberal/ environmentalist states such as California are pursuing unilateral steps to reduce their own carbon emissions. Ten Northeastern and Mid-Atlantic states have committed to reduce their $CO_2$ emissions from the power sector 10 percent by 2018. In 2006 California enacted AB32, which commits California to reducing its greenhouse gas emissions by 20 percent below the 1990s level by the year 2020 and by 80 percent by the year 2050. Many details still have to be worked out, but this regulation stands out as a credible commitment to decarbonize the state's economy. Both federal and state carbon regulation will have significant effects on several sectors of our economy.

## Coal

Given our nation's current reliance on cheap coal-fired power plants, such carbon regulation will lead to higher electricity prices. At the national level in 2004, the average power plant emitted 1,358 pounds of carbon dioxide per megawatt hour, and 48 percent of our total power generation came from coal-fired powered plants. This average masks broad variation across the states. For example, California's average emissions factor was 697 pounds per megawatt hour, whereas Indiana's was 2,091 pounds per megawatt hour. In Midwestern states such as Ohio and Missouri, coal-fired power plants are responsible for over 86 percent of the total electricity production. Residents of such states have a strong financial incentive to oppose legislation that will raise the price of consuming power generated from coal. A carbon permit price of $50 per ton of carbon dioxide is predicted to raise the price of gasoline by 26 percent, the price of residential natural gas by 25 percent, and the price of coal by a much larger percentage.[10]

In the short run, such higher energy prices will impose costs as energy-intensive industries face higher costs of production. Eventually this pollution tax will foster increased reliance on power generation using renewables such as wind and solar power.

## Ships and Trains

Consider the trucking industry. Its average fleet fuel economy is roughly 6.5 miles per gallon—so traveling 1,000 miles requires 154 gallons of gasoline. At $3 a gallon, this costs $462. If carbon dioxide emissions are priced at $25 per ton, then gas prices would rise by 50 cents per gallon.[11] If gasoline costs $3 per gallon (pre–carbon tax), the price of gas could increase by as much as 16 percent. In contrast, freight trains achieve over 400 mpg using diesel fuel.

Carbon pricing and ongoing fears of "peak oil" (that we are exhausting our finite supplies of gasoline) create strong incentives for companies willing to experiment and offer versions of their products that economize on more expensive natural resources. The ongoing growth of China and India will actually help to improve our economy's energy efficiency. Rising world demand for gasoline raises the likelihood of rising gasoline prices. The expectation of rising oil prices stimulates the demand for more fuel-efficient vehicles, and profit-maximizing producers will oblige by supplying such vehicles. Given that China is an oil importer, its citizens are likely to also demand fuel-efficient vehicles, which offers the possibility of an enormous market for companies that can successfully produce them. The prospect of billions of dollars in profits will lure entrepreneurs to seek out new solutions to our pressing problems. If gasoline prices rise high enough, due to both carbon taxes and the growth of private motor-ization in the developing world, then even Dick Cheney will buy such a green vehicle. (He would not buy it because of any inherent environmentalism but simply to minimize the operating costs of running a vehicle.)

Although large quantities of goods are now shipped by airplane and trucks, in the past waterways and railroads were major shipping routes. It is not an accident that every large city in 1900 was located on a waterway. Of the twenty largest cities in America in 1900, seven were ocean ports where rivers meet the sea (Boston, Providence, New York, Jersey City, Newark, Baltimore, and San Francisco), five were ports where rivers meet the Great Lakes (Milwaukee, Chicago, Detroit, Cleveland, and Buffalo), three were on the Mississippi River (Minneapolis, St. Louis, and New Orleans), three were on the Ohio River (Louisville, Cincinnati, and Pittsburgh), and the remaining two were on east coast rivers, close to the Atlantic Ocean (Philadelphia and Washington).[12]

Carbon pricing will provide incentives to rediscover that past. As the price of shipping goods using trucks and air freight rises, railroads will gain a greater shipping market share, and this will create jobs and opportunities along railroad lines. It is possible that by the middle of the twenty-first century carbon taxes could be $100 per ton. If carbon taxes do rise this high, this would be the equivalent of placing a $2-per-gallon tax on gasoline. In such a post-carbon economy, goods will be less likely to be shipped by truck and more likely to be shipped by rail and waterways. A market test of this claim is offered by Warren Buffet's November 2009 investment of over $30 billion in Burlington Northern Santa Fe railroads.[13] He has made correct investments before, and I am eager to see if this one pays off. If carbon-pricing legislation is enacted, rail freight volumes will rise, and Warren Buffett may become a wealthy man yet again! "It's an all-in wager on the economic future of the United States," he said in a written statement. "I love these bets."

## The Birth of the Hydrogen Hummer

The transportation sector accounts for 40 percent of California's greenhouse gas emissions. California's AB32 will sharply raise fuel economy standards so that new vehicles will average roughly 38 miles per gallon (today the corporate average fuel economy standard for the nation is 27.5 mpg). By setting aggressive fuel economy requirements, my liberal/environmentalist state is engaging in "technology forcing." Given current technologies, we know that smaller vehicles (like golf carts) can be quite fuel efficient. Soon, due to carbon mitigation regulation, Californians who want to drive a big, powerful vehicle will have more trouble finding a new version of such a Hummer to purchase. This could annoy California's governor. It has been reported that he owns seven Hummers. AB32 effectively says, "Hasta la vista, Hummer."

For a Prius lover, the inability to purchase a new gas-guzzling Hummer is no loss, and perhaps it gives them joy to know that the hogs will be denied their tanks. But for those households that love gas guzzlers, the inability to purchase such new vehicles in the future is a cost of this regulation.

Technological innovation can ease this problem. If smart engineers could design a hydrogen Hummer, Arnold Schwarzenegger could have the best of both worlds, enjoying his tanks while releasing zero carbon emissions. Carbon pricing and a social media campaign celebrating the virtuousness of owning such a vehicle will stimulate demand for it. Sufficient demand for the hydrogen Hummer would increase the likelihood that some smart future entrepreneur will succeed in developing it. If Arnold is the only person who seeks out a hydrogen Hummer, no nerd will waste time developing this costly product for such a small market. The irony here is that Arnold needs to clone himself many, many times so that he can be happy in the future carbon-constrained world. That sounds like the plot of one of his movies.

## Jobs

Anti-carbon regulations will simultaneously create and destroy jobs. Older, energy-intensive manufacturing firms may face much higher costs of doing business, and this may lead them to shut down or seek out international locations featuring lower electricity prices and less stringent carbon regulation. In my recent research I have investigated whether manufacturing employers migrate away from areas with high electricity prices. Abstracting from some details, my punch line is that only a handful of energy-intensive industries like primary metal manufacturing and textile mills are responsive to high electricity prices. These industries avoid high electricity price areas, but there are others such as paper manufacturing that are not responsive to electricity prices.

Higher energy prices induced by the anti-carbon regulations will retard growth in a couple of manufacturing industries, but these same regulations will act to stimulate new manufacturing opportunities in a variety of industries, ranging from energy-efficient household appliances, to solar panels, to energy-efficient vehicles. Where will these new green industries cluster? They might go to a high-tech state like California or a low-wage one like Mississippi. The answer hinges on what the key inputs in the production process are. If solar panels are mass produced and are labor intensive to produce, then such panels will be produced in right to work (anti-union) states where labor is relatively inexpensive. If green technology is knowledge intensive, such firms will locate in superstar cities close to leading universities.

## GREEN JOBS AS AN URBAN GROWTH STRATEGY

Today, unemployment is high in center-city Detroit. If new jobs are created there, will these jobs go to the urban unemployed who currently live there? Economists have documented a surprising fact. For every one hundred new jobs created in a city, only a small share of jobs (less than 10 percent) go to unemployed residents. The bulk of the new jobs go to new migrants who have recently moved into the city. This could be a mixture of international immigrants and domestic migrants. A Detroit mayor who cares about the incumbent unemployed would be frustrated if their quality of life does not improve as the city's fortunes improve. In an extreme case, Detroit could enjoy a renaissance, but the unemployed in Detroit would not gain much. Land prices would rise, and in an extreme case rents as well, and wages and employment prospects would not improve, so the quality of life of the poorest would actually be made worse by the economic recovery of the region.

The Obama administration has embraced best-selling author Van Jones's idea to kill two birds with one green stone. By using public-sector funds to subsidize urban minorities to get training and jobs in the green economy, the goal is to simultaneously reduce minority unemployment in major cities and reduce our carbon footprint. Jones has created Green For All, as part of the Clean Energy Corps Working Group. He has launched a campaign for a Clean Energy Corps initiative, which hopes to create 600,000 green-collar jobs while retrofitting and upgrading more than 15 million American buildings.[14] In September 2009 Jones resigned from the Obama administration, but his ideas have been eagerly embraced by the president.

The January 12, 2009, issue of the *New Yorker* contained a long profile of Jones. Few economists receive this treatment.[15] Perhaps because the author of the piece, Elizabeth Kolbert, needed some skepticism to balance Mr. Jones's optimism, she asked me to comment on his program. Kolbert wrote, "Matthew Kahn, an economics professor at U.C.L.A.'s Institute of the Environment, noted that public-works programs have a history of inefficiency. Why would an environmentally oriented public-works program be any different? 'How do we make sure this isn't just a giant green boondoggle?' he asked."[16] Honestly, I enjoyed playing the devil's advocate here. My mother was proud to see me quoted in the *New Yorker* and was also impressed that I was called by Elizabeth Kolbert, one of her heroes. Everybody won. (Yet the magazine continues to reject my entries in its cartoon caption contest.)

In the midst of a deep recession, John Maynard Keynes has been rehabilitated, and it has become politically correct to support an FDR-style "Green New Deal," but I worry that an enormous green public works campaign could create one million green "Newmans" from *Seinfeld*. For those who did not watch this show during the 1990s, Newman was the lazy postman who was well aware that he had a cushy sinecure— he fully abused his lifetime employment by delivering as little mail as possible (and even storing bags of other people's mail in his apartment).

The public sector is not known for its productivity. Cynical economists have argued that the compressed pay scale and the difficulties in firing public-sector employees lead to shirking and slacking off. Unlike in a professional golf tournament (where the first-place prize can be twice as big as the second-place prize), there is little incentive to try hard. If the cynics are right, an unintended consequence of this well-meaning program will be a bloated payroll of workers who are not cost-effectively increasing America's energy efficiency.

The Van Jones vision would encourage the Obama administration to offer large lump sum grants to urban areas to train workers with skills to "green" the economy. His approach is to encourage supply-side policies that train a new generation of workers with specific skills. Job training sounds good on paper, but evaluations of the 1980s Jobs Training Partnership Act (JTPA) yielded disappointingly low estimates of the gains from participating in such programs.[17]

We all agree that reducing our greenhouse gas emissions and improving the quality of life of the urban poor are both worthy goals. There is a continuing policy disagreement on how to achieve these aims. A carbon tax would directly achieve both. Such an explicit incentive would encourage all greenhouse gas producers to take a second look at their day-to-day activities and try to identify wasteful practices. For example, a homeowner might be shocked at his or her new summer electricity bill once electricity prices reflect the embedded carbon emissions. Similarly, winter fuel bills in New England, where households heat with oil and natural gas, would be larger due to carbon pricing. In both cases, homeowners would have a strong incentive to call in the weatherizers to look for ways to improve the home's energy efficiency. Such firms would seek to hire an active staff to conduct these house calls.

### NEW GREEN TECH CORRIDORS

In California today, the Golden State is trying to figure out what the next big wave of growth will be based on. It is unlikely to be moviemaking or military contracts or orange growing. Many hope that "green tech" will offer this state its next major growth sector. California has great universities, access to venture capital, an active environmentalist population, and a government willing to enact "pro-green" policies, but it is competing against other states with cheaper labor and more business-friendly regulations. Economists continue to ponder why certain industrial clusters take root in certain areas. In brief, why is (was?) Wall Street on Wall Street? Why is Silicon Valley in Silicon Valley?

In the case of Silicon Valley, its proximity to Stanford and UC Berkeley offers it easy access to a talented labor pool (undergraduates and graduate students) and ready access to the faculty of each of these universities, who act as part-time consultants. That's the same reason Google China is near Tsinghua University. The high quality of life of the area in terms of amenities and weather creates a centripetal force that attracts more skilled people to live there. This in turn attracts venture capitalists and other deal makers to live nearby to network and to learn about what "hot" new products are in development. To be able to learn in the high-amenity environment of California is a unique opportunity.

Cities with leading research universities have an edge in attracting these new green clusters. At the start of this movement to decarbonize our economy, companies will learn from others within their industry and located nearby. Anticipating this point, new green startup firms will want to locate near other firms they can learn from. Cities such as Boston, with leading engineering schools, will have an advantage in attracting these firms to locate nearby.

As various cities pursue the first mover advantage—the idea that those who adopt new ideas first enjoy a big jump on the competition—of offering incentives to become the "green tech" capital, they face the fundamental challenge of picking winners.[18] All over the world, governments have a bad record in picking industrial winners. People point to

Japan's MITI (Ministry of International Trade and Industry) as an example of successful activist government management of strategic subsidies, but economists who bother to study the performance of subsidized companies compared to industries and firms that did not receive such preferential treatment have been unimpressed with the rate of return on these public investments.[19]

Picking winners is a costly business. All over the United States, cities have experimented with offering targeted subsidies to keep certain key "anchor" businesses. In New York City, the mayor will build a new sports stadium to keep the New York Yankees or offer Goldman Sachs special tax incentives to remain in Manhattan. When cities get into a bidding war with other cities to attract a new factory, they suffer from what economists call the winner's curse. Here's how it works: Consider a jar of jelly beans. Let ten people independently bid for the jelly beans by writing down a bid (in dollars) on a sheet of paper. Nobody observes anybody else's bid. If I sell the jelly beans to the person who bids the most, the winner is likely to have overbid and thus suffer the winner's curse. The winning bid will be the highest of the bids, but the best guess of the true value of the jelly beans will be the average bid. The winner overpaid! The same logic applies in the case of the new factory when cities bid against each other to have it locate within their borders. Before the factory is built, it is unknown what its value to a city will be. The winning bidder is likely to overpay for the factory.

## *Star Trek* Now

We are starting to see surprising new entrants into the green game. Consider the new city of Masdar, Abu Dhabi. This oil-rich nation is designing a city of the future. The construction is the start of a vast experiment, an attempt to create the world's first car-free, zero-carbon-dioxide-emissions, zero-waste city. Due to be completed in 2016, the city is the centerpiece of the Masdar Initiative, a $15-billion investment by the government of Abu Dhabi, which is part of the United Arab Emirates. The new development, being built on the outskirts of Abu Dhabi city, will run almost entirely on energy from the sun and will use just 20 percent as much power as a conventional city of similar size.

A major goal in the construction of Masdar City is for it to act as a guinea pig for developing better future "zero-impact" cities. The city is intended to generate as much electricity as it uses. Garbage will be sorted and recycled or used for compost; sewage will be processed into fuel.

> Its water will be recycled to save the energy costs of desalination. Vacuum tubes under the city will transport garbage to a central location, where it will be sorted, and as much as possible will be recycled. Trash that can't be recycled will be converted to energy through a gasification process and the leftovers incorporated into building materials. Sewage will be treated and some of it processed into a dry renewable fuel for generating electricity. A small fraction of the energy that's still needed to run the city will come from waste-based fuel and perhaps geothermal power.

The rest will come from the sun—but not all of it through expensive photovoltaics, which convert sunlight into electricity.[20]

Abu Dhabi is not alone. China is starting to build a small ecocity, Dongtan.[21] To be built on land close to Shanghai, by 2040 the city is slated to be one-third the size of Manhattan, with a total planned population of 500,000—but no construction has yet taken place, so the project has fallen behind schedule. Teaming with a British engineering firm, China's goal is to build a city planned to be ecologically friendly, with zero-greenhouse-emission transit and complete self-sufficiency in water and energy, together with the use of zero-energy building principles. Energy demand will be substantially lower than in comparable conventional cities due to the high performance of buildings and a zero-emission transport zone within the city. Waste is considered to be a resource, and most of the city's waste will be recycled.

This utopian city has not actually been built yet. But the cases of both Abu Dhabi and China highlight that nations that do not have a history of environmental progressivism are pursuing a diversified business strategy as they anticipate a carbon-constrained future. In a globalized world economy, those nations that can gain a competitive edge in producing "green products" will enjoy a growth in exports and an increase in their population's standard of living. Opportunity knocks.

# 9

# THE FUTURE OF CITIES

nlike humans, birds, butterflies, camels, and sharks live outside. Most do not have access to food storage and must spend a big chunk of their day searching for it. Unlike humans, they cannot buy a bus ticket and move to a better geographical location that offers their favorite temperature and food opportunities.

Climate change will almost certainly cause extreme dislocation for many ecosystems as they experience changes in rainfall and temperature. Ecologists are measuring the speed that different animals, birds, and plants can move. Intuitively, if you are fast you can move a greater distance, and then you can find your new favorite location in our hotter world.

In the case of birds, a rise in temperature will push them to seek out higher elevations. A study of twenty-six mountains in Switzerland documented that alpine flora have expanded toward the summits since the plots were first measured in the 1940s. The researchers noted, "Upward movement of treelines has been observed in Siberia and in the Canadian Rocky Mountains, where temperatures have risen by 1.5 degrees C. In Spain, the lower elevational limits of 16 species of butterfly have risen an average of 212 meters in 30 years, concurrent with a 1.3 degrees C rise in mean annual temperatures."[1]

Another group of ecologists examined the geography of small mammals who live in California's Yosemite National Park. An earlier researcher named Joseph Grinnell had surveyed these creatures between 1914 and 1920. The modern researchers studied whether small mammals have remained where Grinnell previously found them. The mice have moved. Creatures like the pocket mouse, the California vole, and the harvest mouse have all migrated to higher elevations between 1920 and today.[2] Are they just as happy in their new habitats? A future sociologist may be able to answer that question, but it is clear to me that these creatures are acting in their own self-interest to protect themselves in our hotter world.

Evolution has prepared some creatures for climate change. Great white sharks swim across vast distances. Scientists spent eight years tracking the movements of 179 great white sharks and discovered that these predators have predictable migration patterns between Hawaii and the North American coast (San Francisco).[3] The camel is also ready for change. It can store large quantities of water in its hump, and this protects it from prolonged periods of not being able to find water. Its long eyelashes protect it from wind storms.[4]

But birds and voles will find that mountains are finite, thus limiting their opportunities to adapt. Ecologists bemoan the fragmented land patterns caused by roads and suburban development, which interfere with migration. Today we have dedicated nature preserves that allow creates to live in their own area, but climate change may strip from such areas the climate conditions that they have evolved to live in. Humans can migrate, but animals will not be welcome in areas where people want to live. In this sense, our cities and our adaptation to climate change will interfere with the evolutionary ability of other species to adapt to climate change.

So seemingly we have a leg up on the rest of the creatures that inhabit this planet: our ability to innovate gets us out of jams that we created for ourselves. Of course it takes time to come up with and implement such visions, but the power to think ahead and anticipate does distinguish us from other creatures. In a diverse society, if only 1 percent of us are forward-looking Mr. Spocks and the rest of us are like Homer Simpson, then the first group will grow quite rich as they create the products and opportunities that allow us Homers to get through the night as climate change affects us.

We do not need every member of society to anticipate climate change's impacts and spend all day tinkering around in the garage, trying to build highly energy-efficient air conditioners and water desalinization processes. Instead, we just need a fraction of the best minds in our world of 7 billion people to tackle these problems, and we must give them enough time (thirty years until climate change's blows really start) and resources (venture capitalists wanting to simultaneously get rich and protect the planet). Not all of these ventures will succeed, but the very best efforts will offer us not only the next Toyota Prius but other excellent products that help us adapt to climate change. This means that we will never end up like Mel Gibson in *Mad Max*, fighting lunatics for the last gallon of gasoline in a declining world. Or like the California vole, looking for ever-higher ecosystems.

But it's undeniable that in cities around the world, climate change threatens to cause destruction to physical capital and to kill and destroy. Given our taste for living in coastal areas, we have collectively chosen to put ourselves at risk from significant sea level rise. The private insurance industry dreads the possibility of two different climate change–induced "triple witching hours." In one case, heat waves directly cause death and fires and exacerbate local air pollution, which will kill some people, whose families will then collect on life insurance policies.[5] In the second case, climate change will increase the frequency of severe hurricanes and cause sea level rise. When such a hurricane occurs at high tide during a time of rising sea levels, the coastal impacts will be truly scary.

Naturally, the late-night comics have voiced their thoughts on this issue:

"Yesterday, a group of scientists warned that because of global warming, sea levels will rise so much that parts of New Jersey will be under water. The bad news? Parts of New Jersey won't be under water."

—CONAN O'BRIEN

"Scientists say because of global warming they expect the world's oceans to rise four and a half feet. The scientists say this can mean only one thing: Gary Coleman is going to drown."

—CONAN O'BRIEN

"Experts say this global warming is serious, and they are predicting now that by the year 2050, we will be out of party ice."

—DAVID LETTERMAN

Climate change poses risks that are easy to joke about but difficult to quantify. We simply do not know how world aggregate greenhouse gas production affects the climate. We also do not know how much cumulative greenhouse gases the world will produce in the future. There are many possible future scenarios showing how hot it may be in the year 2100.

Despite these challenges, I am highly optimistic about the quality of life in our future cities. During one 1980 presidential campaign debate, Ronald Reagan famously asked the American people, "Are you better off than you were four years ago?" The electorate answered with a resounding "no," and voted Reagan into office over the hapless incumbent, Jimmy Carter. When we ask the same question in 2050, very few of us will want to go back to the bad old days of the twentieth century. Over the next hundred years, the world's population and per capita income will both continue to grow. Fueled by urbanization, much of this growth will take place in developing countries. This spread of the "American Dream" to more and more people all over the world offers great opportunities that many of us in rich countries take for granted.

Credible carbon mitigation efforts would make me even more confident about this prediction, but I am not surprised that the world has been slow to embrace sacrifice for the greater good. After all, regulating carbon emissions is not a free lunch. It involves accepting costs today (such as higher gasoline and electricity prices) in return for a less risky future. Impatient people and people who have trouble imagining such a future are unlikely to accept this offer.

Adaptation is a different kettle of fish. Because we directly bear the costs of climate change's impacts, we have the right incentives to take actions to protect ourselves. As our cities experience changing climate conditions and increased risk of natural disasters, self-interested households will take a variety of steps to protect their health, property, and quality of life. The narrow pursuit of self-interest is an old theme in economics. Although some may call it selfish, the eighteenth-century economist Adam Smith would disagree: "It is not from the benevolence of the butcher, the brewer, or the baker that we expect our dinner, but from their regard to their own interest." Recall the discussion in chapter 2 about Thom Mayne, the UCLA architect who is designing homes that can float on flood waters. He anticipates that self-interested house-holds will demand his novel homes. I have never met him; it is possible that mere altruism drives his desire to produce this new product. But just as in the case of Google (whose motto is "Don't be evil"), the billions of dollars of potential profit don't hurt in motivating individuals such as Mayne to consider new strategies for helping others to cope in our hotter world.

## Forecasting Our Future

A skeptic might suggest that an economist who is optimistic about our future needs new glasses. After all, economists did not anticipate the deep recession of 2008 and 2009. It seems like only yesterday that Alan Greenspan was viewed as a god, and macro-economists strutted around declaring that we would never suffer from a deep recession again because we had figured out the science of how to manage business cycles. Economists have been humbled by recent events.

Despite our newfound modesty, there is a fundamental difference between predicting stock market dynamics and business cycles and predicting how people will respond to evolving forecasts of future climate scenarios. Nobody can accurately predict future stock prices. If somebody tells you that he has a good idea what the Dow Jones Industrial Average will be on July 7, 2015, or claims to know what the price of Google will be on that date, you should be suspicious. If he knows that the price will go up, then he should be buying now at the low price so that he will become rich. If enough people have access to his information, then their collective stock buying will bid up stock prices so that today's prices will reflect this optimism about the company's future profits. Put briefly, today's stock price will reflect all available current information about the stock's future profitability. So any change in the stock price between now and July 7, 2015, will be caused by new information that is currently not known. Which is to say, stock picking is a fool's game.

Contrast predicting future climate scenarios for a given city such as Los Angeles or London with predicting future stock prices. As climate modelers make progress in their research, they will be increasingly confident about their ability to predict future climate scenarios. These improved forecasts will act as an early warning system, helping households make plans as they become more aware of changing climate conditions in cities they currently live in and in cities they are considering moving to. Recall the Mariel boatlift example discussed in chapter 2. In that case, the Miami population was surprised by the Cuban immigration. But suppose that the Miami population had been tipped off one year before the immigration took place that a huge influx of Cubans was about to move in. With that information, some people in Miami could have moved before the boatlift arrived. The net effect of this anticipatory response would have been that the city would have suffered less dislocation from the boatlift shock.

In the case of adapting to climate change, improved forecasts will offer "new news" to urbanites, which will have profound effects on migration patterns and real estate prices across cities. For example, if climate models predict that Los Angeles summers will be 115 degrees F starting in the year 2050 and we believe this, home prices today in Los Angeles will drop in anticipation of this event. Nobody will build new homes in Los Angeles as the doomsday of 2050 starts to approach. People, such as my family, who bought Los Angeles real estate before this nasty climate forecast became public knowledge, will suffer a huge drop in our asset's value. Anticipating the heat in 2050, Los Angeles's major universities, such as UCLA and USC, could make plans to abandon the city. In the year 2050, I will be an active eighty-four-year-old professor at UCLA. If UCLA chooses to "beat the heat" by moving to a cooler part of California, I would suffer an asset loss (my home would be worth much less than today), but my family would escape physical harm.

In this extreme example, I have assumed that we do have high-quality models of future flood, heat wave, and drought risk, and that the population believes the forecasts. If a segment of the population does not believe these forecasts, then they will buy the Playboy Mansion for $50,000 in the year 2049 and be very unhappy if the forecast turns out to be true in 2050. But they can say to themselves, "There is always a chance that the forecasters are wrong. At worst, I'm out $50,000 for having the option to live in this great house, and if the forecasters are wrong or if the engineers can figure out a technological fix, then I have made the greatest investment in the world."

Consider a less extreme city-specific forecast. Suppose that the climate models predict that Phoenix will soon suffer from severe drought. There are two ways that the people of Phoenix can respond. They can either vote with their feet and leave Phoenix, or they can use the political process to push for collective solutions to more efficiently use existing resources, such as raising water prices to reduce demand for this increasingly scarce resource. The anticipation that the future supply of water will dry up provides an early warning system that encourages early conservation and demand-side responses. The net effect of this early forecast is that Phoenix remains a viable city despite climate change, because the forecasts trigger early responses.

## Optimism

Diet Dr. Pepper and iPods are relatively new products that do not help us adapt to climate change, but their existence highlights the evolutionary nature of capitalism. These products were costly to produce and bring to market. Dr. Pepper was first nationally marketed in 1904, and Diet Dr. Pepper was first sold only recently. For-profit companies will develop such niche products when their marketing research indicates that there is sufficient demand to at least cover the up-front costs of developing the new product. For example, suppose that I suffer from a skin rash and would be willing to pay $1,000 a year for a new ointment that would reduce my pain. If I am the only one in the world who suffers from this problem, no drug company will pay the millions up front to develop the cream to solve my problem. In contrast, if there are millions of people like me, then the for-profit firms will have every incentive to jump in and develop the ointment. The scale of demand for new products encourages firms to evolve their product mix and creates new opportunities for the "next Google." In the near future, climate change will increase demand for products such as energy-efficient air conditioners and water desalinization plants. Such demand will foster new innovations. Adam Smith might call this the "green invisible hand."

For capitalism to protect us from climate change, we must face higher prices for goods and services that will grow scarcer because of the changing climate. Rising prices create strong incentives for buyers to consume less and for sellers to find more and find new substitutes. Globalized energy and food markets help to send out the right signals about what is actually scarce in our growing world economy.

There will be no one magic bullet or key superman such as a General Douglas MacArthur or Mayor Rudi Giuliani to command us to victory against climate change. Adaptation will take place through billions of small choices made by self-interested "no names." To conserve on water, suburbanites will rip out their grass, and urbanites will live in high-rise buildings closer to public transit. Insurance companies will charge different prices for the same housing policy in different locations, and this will send good signals about where people should and should not live within a city. Water agencies will increasingly price water at its true cost of delivery. More resource-efficient products will be offered by for-profit firms as they smell an emerging demand for such products.

Climate change will highlight capitalism's evolutionary ability to cope with change. At the end of the day, there is a delicious irony that capitalist growth has caused the problem of climate change. It has allowed populations to grow and cities to thrive, but it will also protect us from the wrath of climate change's consequences.

In a world where ideas are our scarce resource, the very best ideas from the very best labs create new products that all of us can enjoy. Billions of people use Google today. It is not a unique asset only accessible by the rich and powerful. In a diverse society, we just need a subset of our focused innovation leaders to create products that help us adapt to climate change. Once they exist, even Homer Simpson will purchase them. Such products are more likely to be developed and marketed if there is a market for adaptation.

## Spin and the Culture Wars

Optimism in the face of climate change is not politically correct. I understand that the fear of coming doom helps those (including myself) who support carbon taxes today argue that we need to adopt costly mitigation policies (like the gasoline tax and other carbon taxes).

At the start of 2010, the U.S. Senate shows no signs of passing a serious carbon mitigation bill. It is clear that senators representing states in high-carbon-producing, conservative areas such as Missouri are much less willing to vote in favor of costly regulation than senators from liberal, low-carbon-producing states such as California.[6] Missouri senators are more likely to vote in favor of carbon mitigation regulation if they expect their constituents to suffer significant future pain caused by climate change. This anticipation would create an "urgency of now" that helps to overcome our desire to delay pain and costly sacrifice.

I do not intend for this book to lull moderates into thinking that "since we can adapt, we don't need to mitigate." I also would not be delighted if polluting interest groups such as coal-fired electric utilities pointed to this book and said, "This guy says that we have nothing to worry about in our hotter future. So why are we raising business costs by pushing to reduce carbon emissions and moving toward unproven, costly renewable electricity?"

Reducing carbon emissions now will make the future challenge to adapt easier to face. Collectively, we as a society need to take a sober look at the tradeoffs. What will it cost us now to reduce our carbon emissions? Who within our society (the rich, the poor, people from the Rust Belt?) will pay the bulk of this new carbon tax? We must trade off these costs of carbon mitigation against less sea level rise and smaller temperature increases. Obviously this is a very difficult question to resolve, but I reject the extreme view that our cities are doomed if we allow climate change to play out. Some physical places will suffer greatly, but mobile urbanites will continue to thrive.

## Do Economists Love Cities Too Much?

An ecologist who reads this book might label it as narrow. As the share of people living in the countryside all over the world shrinks, urban interests will drive national mitigation and adaptation policies. But I realize that the vast majority of the world's creatures that will be affected by climate change do not live in my study area. I have focused on just a single set of creatures that are part of the homo sapiens species. These creatures (we) are messing with Mother Nature through creating too much greenhouse gases, and we do not fully understand the web of nature and its feedbacks and interconnections. Some critics may argue that a well-written book might lull readers into a false sense of confidence about our future by focusing on physical areas (cities) that are built to minimize contact with the natural world. After all, urbanites live and work inside and as of now do not have to hunt for food.

By focusing on cities, where there are billions of people but there is not much land or biodiversity, I am explicitly embracing an economist's "human centric" bias. If people are happy and believe that their standard of living is improving, we economists declare that society is making progress. Of course progress should not be based solely on perceptions of quality of life. Typically, especially around election time, the health of the economy is the key determinant for how we are doing. All economists know that national growth in per capita income is not a great indicator of progress. Brilliant economists such as the Nobel Laureates Joe Stiglitz and Amartya Sen continue to wrestle with how to incorporate nonmarket goods such as a clean environment and leisure opportunities into national accounts.[7]

If we as a society declare that our only goal is to maximize our average household income, then climate change is unlikely to be a major future threat. The U.S. economy is now a services and high-skill economy. Think of Google. Could climate change really wipe out Google and its workers' productivity? If the firm at its present headquarters in northern California was affected by unexpected shocks, it could relocate to a safer location in South Dakota. There would be losers from this move (landowners near the current Google headquarters) and winners (those who own land in South Dakota). Although I do not believe that climate change will dislocate our overall economy's well-being, I have presented throughout this book a series of examples of how it will greatly affect our quality of life if we continue with business as usual. We will face extra risk of flooding, drought, heat waves, and pollution.

## The Food Chain

I recognize that urbanites are dependent on rural areas for basic food supplies. Many researchers today are investigating how climate change will affect the agricultural sector. Development economists are worried about future scenarios in which there are billions more people, who due to income growth are seeking more calories at the same time that climate change impinges on the productivity of rural agriculture.

But a key theme in modern economics is that our scarcest resource is human ingenuity, not natural capital. On August 24, 2009, the *New York Times* featured an op-ed piece by Dickson D. Despommier, an ecologist at Columbia University, titled "A Farm on Every Floor." He sketched his vision of the future of farming in cities. By definition, farms need land, but Despommier wants to "go vertical." He would place farming activity in skyscrapers! In vertical farming, wind turbines and solar panels would power a building devoted to farming that would economize on the carbon footprint, chemicals, and water use. Bloggers have quickly jumped in and called this idea nuts based on alternative uses for land in expensive cities such as New York City. One back-of-the-envelope calculation priced "urban farmland" at between $13 million and $43 million per acre and argued that the broccoli that it would yield had better taste extremely good.[8]

Land in cities such as Manhattan is quite expensive, but in other cities, such as Detroit, it is not. So vertical farming might be worth trying in Detroit. If it works there, it would spread. Despommier's idea highlights the possibility that food could be grown in very different settings than it currently is. He has voiced an optimistic vision of how we can change our ways and grow food in our hotter world.

## My Doubts?

Throughout this book, I have taken it for granted that the risk of serious climate change is real and that its effects in this century will unfold in a gradual fashion. I admit that much of my optimism goes out the window if climate change inflicts abrupt shocks. If sea levels unexpectedly rise 3 feet in a month near New York City, there is nothing that the residents of southern Manhattan can do to protect themselves.

This book has devoted no time to the claim that climate change is not taking place. Ecologists have devoted their careers to examining the geographical distributions of where different creatures live and documenting the "coincidental patterns" showing that many creatures have been on the move, seeking out more hospitable climate conditions in a hotter world. I have taken it for granted that humans are next.

It is possible that I am a Chicken Little, scaring people about a phony threat. Climate skeptics argue that a vast left-wing conspiracy has dreamed up the climate change issue to nudge the Hummer crowd to live a more politically correct lifestyle (featuring tofu rather than red meat, bikes rather than cars, and solar panels) while simultaneously creating a vast federal funding justification for the research grants that the researchers covet.

But I would be more than a little shocked if the year 2100 rolls around and none of the major predictions made by the climate change modelers today, involving rising average temperatures, significant sea level rise, shifts in the intensity of natural disasters, and changes in precipitation and drought conditions, has come to pass. If this future unfolds, I would gladly pay for Rush Limbaugh to have a seven-course red meat meal at any restaurant he picks.

But even if I'm wrong, we lose little by being aware of a potential threat posed by the fossil fuel–intensive lifestyle that we have relied on for so long. If I truly am a Chicken Little who is dead wrong about the future quality-of-life challenges in coastal cities, and if these cities do take strong steps such as zoning off growth in at-risk places and investing more to strengthen infrastructure, then these investments will be considered "wasteful." We could have continued to thrive without taking these steps. This is like buying life insurance at the age of fifty-five. If you are alive at the age of ninety, you have "wasted" thirty-five years' worth of life insurance premiums when you didn't need to (you didn't die). But at the time, this action provided you peace of mind. The typical person is highly risk averse.

In the case of climate change, my optimism is in part based on the belief that we will not be paralyzed by fear but instead will seize the day and be proactive. I am concerned about how the urban poor in both rich and poor nations will cope with climate change, but the truth is that this group has always faced hardship. To a cold-hearted economist, the question is *how much worse* will their quality of life be in the face of climate change? An optimist would say that climate change will create an imperative for nations to embrace pro-growth strategies to help their poor move up the economic ladder. If such nations could grow by 3 percent per year for the next sixty years, then millions of people in these countries would escape poverty, giving them their own resources to make choices that would help their families cope in a hotter world.

Unlike the Manhattan Project during World War II, we do not need to make one big bet on *the* strategy for winning this war. Instead, we will launch a billion mutinies against climate change. In a world with billions of educated, ambitious individuals, the best adaptations and innovations will be pretty good.

# ACKNOWLEDGMENTS

I am indebted to many friends and colleagues who have taught me about how climate change will affect our quality of life. My colleagues at the Fletcher School at Tufts University and at the UCLA Institute of the Environment have greatly influenced my views. I am also grateful to my colleagues at the National Bureau of Economic Research's Environmental and Energy Economics Program. This group brings together some of the nation's leading empirical economists to discuss research at the frontier.

This book was written at UCLA. The Westwood campus's sunshine has been good for my productivity and my tan. UCLA's excellent students have pushed me in the classroom to refine and clarify my thinking. Their collective feedback has helped to sharpen this book's core themes.

I could not have written this book without the help of my editor, Tim Sullivan. While I suffer from waves of "irrational exuberance" about the quality of my own work, Tim knows how to give me the "inconvenient truth." When coming from Tim, I can handle the truth, and his calm advice always pushes me to not be complacent and to work harder.

This book is dedicated to my wife, Dora L. Costa, and our son, Alexander Harry Costa Kahn. When he turns forty-four in the year 2045, I hope that Alex reads this book and smiles as he realizes that his old man was pretty sharp back in the day. I will be seventy-nine then and still trying to turn this book into a movie. That's what we West Los Angeles people really seek. In Los Angeles, people stop and ask my wife whether I am Quentin Tarantino. She says that she is not sure.

# NOTES

## Notes for Chapter 1

1. "Cities in Africa and Asia to Double in Size by 2030: UN Population Fund," http://www.un.org/apps/news/story.asp?NewsID=23060&Cr=world&Cr1=population (accessed March 13, 2010).

2. Arthur H. Westing, "Overpopulation and Climate Change," *New York Times*, February 18, 2010, http://www.nytimes.com/2010/02/18/opinion/1#8iht-edwesting.html (accessed March 13, 2010).

3. "International Energy Outlook," 2009, http://www.eia.doe.gov/oiaf/ieo/highlights.html (accessed March 13, 2010).

4. Paul Krugman, "Boiling the Frog," *New York Times*, July 13, 2009, http://www.nytimes.com/2009/07/13/opinion/13krugman.html (accessed March 13, 2010).

5. "From the Bedroom to the Bomb: An Interview with Paul Ehrlich by Lee Altenberg," *The Stanford Daily*, April 1, 1983, http://dynamics.org/~altenber/PAPERS/EHRLICH/ (accessed March 13, 2010): "But when you make strong statements about the future, what you're hoping to do is mobilize people into action to make them go in some different direction, and I think that's happened faster than I thought it would also."

6. Elizabeth Kolbert, "What Was I Thinking?" *New Yorker*, February 25, 2008, http://rotman.utoronto.ca/nina.mazar/Media/Mazar_NewYorker_ZeroPrice.pdf (accessed March 13, 2010).

7. http://en.wikipedia.org/wiki/Never_was_so_much_owed_by_so_many_to_so_few (accessed March 13, 2010).

## Notes for Chapter 2

1. Jamais Cascio, "Get Smarter," *Atlantic*, July/August 2009, http://www.theatlantic.com/doc/200907/intelligence (accessed March 14, 2010).

2. http://en.wikipedia.org/wiki/Lake_Toba (accessed March 14, 2010).

3. Cascio, "Get Smarter."

4. "Chicago's Recovery," *New York Times*, October 12, 1881, http://query.nytimes.com/mem/archivefree/pdf?res=9A01E5DD103EE433A25751C1A9669D9609FD7CF (accessed March 14, 2010).

5. Guido W. Imbens, Donald B. Rubin, and Bruce I. Sacerdote, 2001. "Estimating the Effect of Unearned Income on Labor Earnings, Savings, and Consumption: Evidence from a Survey of Lottery Players," *American Economic Review* 91, no.4 (September 2001): 778–794.

6. Benjamin F. Jones and Benjamin A. Olken, "Hit or Miss? The Effect of Assassinations on Institutions and War" (Working Paper 13102, National Bureau of Economic Research, May 2007), http://ideas.repec.org/p/nbr/nberwo/13102.html (accessed March 14, 2010).

7. Donald R. Davis and David E. Weinstein, "Bones, Bombs, and Break Points: The Geography of Economic Activity," *American Economic Review* 92, no. 5 (December 2002): 1269–1289.

8. Edward Miguel and Gerard Roland, "The Long Run Impact of Bombing Vietnam" (working paper, University of California at Berkeley, November 2006), http://elsa.berkeley.edu/~emiguel/pdfs/miguel_vietnam.pdf (accessed March 14, 2010).

9.      http://www.zillow.com/homes/for_sale/Troy-NY/#/homes/for_sale/Troy-NY/41292_rid/42.895905,-73.344066,42.593348,-74.010112_rect/9_zm/ (accessed March 14, 2010).

10. http://en.wikipedia.org/wiki/New_Orleans (accessed March 14, 2010).

11. "Federal Coordinator for Gulf Coast Rebuilding Douglas O'Dell Hosts Federal Inspectors General Strategy Meeting" (press release, Department of Homeland Security, May 13, 2008), http://www.dhs.gov/xnews/releases/pr_1210791829291.shtm (accessed March 14, 2010).

12. http://en.wikipedia.org/wiki/Marshall_Plan (accessed March 14, 2010).

13. Population Division, United Nations, "World Population Aging, 1950–2050," http://www.un.org/esa/population/publications/worldageing19502050/pdf/020weste.pdf (accessed March 14, 2010).

14. A determined researcher could quantify this using the data available at http://tvnews.vanderbilt.edu/ (accessed March 14, 2010).

15. David Strömberg and Thomas Eisensee, "News Floods, News Droughts, and U.S. Disaster Relief," *Quarterly Journal of Economics* 122, no. 2 (2007): 693–728.

16. Department of Homeland Security, National Response Framework, January 2008, http://www.fema.gov/pdf/emergency/nrf/nrf-core.pdf (accessed March 14, 2010).

17. http://en.wikipedia.org/wiki/Great_Flood_of_1993 (accessed March 14, 2010).

18. Lee W. Larson, "The Great USA Food of 1993" (paper presented at the IAHS Conference Destructive Water: Water-Caused Natural Disasters—Their Abatement and Control, Anaheim, California, June 24–28, 1996), http://www.nwrfc.noaa.gov/floods/papers/oh_2/great.htm (accessed March 14, 2010).

19. Sarah Shipley, "A Flood of Development: Unprecedented Growth in the Flood Plain Brings Riches and Risks," *St. Louis Post-Dispatch,* July 28, 2003, http://training.fema.gov/EMIweb/edu/docs/hazdem/A%20Flood%20of%20Development%20-%20Unprecedented%20Growth.doc (accessed March 14, 2010).

20. "Ongoing Midwest Flooding Threatens Mississippi River Levees," *PBS Newshour,* June 17, 2008 (transcript),

http://www.pbs.org/newshour/bb/weather/jan-june08/leveetrouble_06–17.html (accessed March 14, 2010).

21. Shipley, "Flood of Development."

22. Meg Sullivan, "UCLA Geographers Urge US to Narrow Search for bin Laden," February 17, 2009, http://www.international.ucla.edu/article.asp?parentid=104836 (accessed March 14, 2010).

23. Institute for Business and Home Safety, "The Benefits of Modern Wind Resistant Buildings Codes on Hurricane Claim Frequency and Severity," August 2004, http://www.disastersafety.org/resource/resmgr/hurricane_charley.pdf (accessed March 14, 2010).

24. Randy E. Dumm, Stacy Sirmans, and Greg Smersh, "The Capitalization of Building Codes in Home Prices," *Journal of Real Estate Finance and Economics* (April 2009). http://www.springerlink.com/content/v301#5077158848g4/ (accessed March 14, 2010).

25. Stacey Plaisance, "Floating House Could Ride New Orleans' Floods," Associated Press, October 9, 2009, http://www.csmonitor.com/Environment/2009/1009/floating-house-could-ride-new-orleans-floods (accessed March 14, 2010).

26. Stacey Plaisance, "House Capable of Floating Debuts in New Orleans," Associated Press, October 10,2009, http://seattletimes.nwsource.com/html/realestate/2010034086_realfloatinghouse11.html (accessed March 14, 2010).

27. http://en.wikipedia.org/wiki/Potter_Palmer (accessed March 14, 2010).

28. "Arthur Charles Ducat Sr.," Arlington National Cemetery Web site, http://www.arlingtoncemetery.net/acducatsr.htm (accessed March 14, 2010).

29. George Raine, "The Great Quake: 1906–2006 Funding the Recovery," *San Francisco Chronicle,* April 14, 2006, http://sfgate.com/cgi-bin/article.cgi?f=/c/a/2006/04/14/BUG5DI8M031.DTL (accessed March 14, 2010).

30. Richard Fausset, "New Orleans Rebuilds, but Along the Same Lines? Reflecting a Racial Divide, Many Fear the City Will Abandon Low-lying Areas; Others Think It Ought To," *LA Times,* May 31, 2009, http://www.latimes.com/news/nationworld/nation/la-na-shrink-new-orleans31–2009may31,0,1428057.story (accessed March 14, 2010).

31. Patrick Sharkey, "Survival and Death in New Orleans: An Empirical Look at the Human Impact of Hurricane Katrina," *Journal of Black Studies* 37 (2007): 482–501, http://sociology.as.nyu.edu/docs/IO/6024/sharkey_Katrina.pdf (accessed March 14, 2010).

32. David Card, "The Impact of the Mariel Boatlift on the Miami Labor Market," *Industrial and Labor Relations Review* 43, no. 2 (1990): 245–257, http://emlab.berkeley.edu/~card/papers/mariel-impact.pdf (accessed March 14, 2010).

33. Ibid.

34. Albert Saiz, "Room in the Kitchen for the Melting Pot: Immigration and Rental Prices," *Review of Economics and Statistics* (August 2003): 502–521.

## Notes for Chapter 3

1. Frank Knight, *Risk, Uncertainty and Profit* (New York: Houghton Mifflin, 1921).

2. "North Dakota Development Land for Sale," http://www.loopnet.com/North-Dakota_Development-Land-For-Sale/ (accessed March 14, 2010).

3. Edward L. Glaeser, Jose A. Scheinkman, and Andrei Shleifer, "Economic Growth in a Cross-section of Cities," *Journal of Monetary Economics* 36, no. 1 (August 1995): 117–143.

4. http://en.wikipedia.org/wiki/Coda_Automotive (accessed March 14, 2010).

5. For more details see the Mayor of London's "The London Plan" at http://www.london.gov.uk/approot/mayor/strategies/sds/london_plan_download.jsp (accessed November 4, 2005).

6. Jordan Rappaport and Jeffrey D. Sachs, "The United States as a Coastal Nation," *Journal of Economic Growth* 8, no. 1 (March 2003): 5–46.

7. Robert J. Nicholls and Richard J. T. Klein, "Climate Change and Coastal Management on Europe's Coast," in *Managing European Coasts: Past, Present, and Future*, ed. J. E. Vermaat et al., 199–225 (Berlin: Springer, 2005), http://www.springerlink.com/content/j7x86g24370780k0/ (accessed March 14, 2010).

8. Steven Messner, Sandra C Miranda, Karen Green, Charles Phillips, Joseph Dudley, Dan Cayan, and Emily Young, "The San Diego Foundation Regional Focus 2050 Study," 2009, http://www.sdfoundation.org/communityimpact/environment/Initiative-focus2050.html (accessed March 14, 2010).

9. U.S. Geological Survey, "Floods: Recurrence Intervals and 100-year Floods," http://ga.water.usgs.gov/edu/100yearflood.html (accessed March 14, 2010).

10. Matthew Heberger, Heather Cooley, Pablo Herrera, Peter H. Gleick, and Eli Moore, "Pacific Institute Report: The Impacts of Sea-Level Rise on the California Coast," May 2009, http://www.pacinst.org/reports/sea_level_rise/report.pdf (accessed March 14, 2010).

11. U.S. Department of Housing and Urban Development, "Moving to Opportunity for Fair Housing," http://portal.hud.gov/portal/page/portal/HUD/programdescription/mto (accessed March 14, 2010).

12. Lawrence Katz, "Moving to Opportunity" (transcript of interview, July 17, 2009), http://www.voxeu.org/index.php?q=node/3768 (accessed March 14, 2010).

13. Justin Rohrlich, "Urban Legends: Bubble Yum Contains Spider Eggs!" August 2, 2009, http://www.minyanville.com/articles/bubble-yum-spider-eggs-urban-legends/index/a/23683 (accessed March 14, 2010).

14. The Preservation Institute, "Removing Freeways, Restoring Cities," 2007, http://www.preservenet.com/freeways/FreewaysHarbor.html (accessed March 14, 2010).

15. Gary Becker and Casey Mulligan, "The Endogenous Determination of Time Preference," *Quarterly Journal of Economics* 112, no. 3 (1997): 729–758.

16. Tiffany Fox, "Regional Study Encourages Immediate Action to Prevent Alarming Effects of Climate Change" (unpublished paper, UC San Diego Sustainability Solutions Institute, December 5, 2008), http://esi.ucsd.edu/esiportal/index.php?option=com_content&task–view&id=223&Itemid=101 (accessed March 14, 2010).

17. Edward L. Glaeser and Matthew E. Kahn, "The Greenness of Cities: Carbon Dioxide Emissions and Urban Development" (Working Paper 14238, National Bureau of Economic Research, 2008).

18. Ibid.

19. http://en.wikipedia.org/wiki/Climate_of_Salt_Lake_City (accessed March 14, 2010).

20. Zack O'Malley Greenburg, "Full List: America's Safest Cities," *Forbes Magazine,* October 26, 2009, http://www.forbes.com/2009/10/26/safest-cities-ten-lifestyle-real-estate-metros-msa_chart.html (accessed March 14, 2010).

21. Steve Doughty, "UK: Number of Britons to Reach 100 Years of Age Hits 10,000," *Daily Mail,* September 18, 2009, http://www.seniorsworldchronicle.com/2009/09/uk-number-of-britons-to-reach-100-years.html (accessed March 14, 2010).

## Notes for Chapter 4

1. Los Angeles County Economic Development Corporation, "Film Industry Profile of California/Los Angeles County," November 29, 2005, http://www.laedc.org/reports/Film-2005.pdf (accessed March 14, 2010).

2. "Americans Spend More Than 100 Hours Commuting to Work Each Year, Census Bureau Reports," *U.S. Census Bureau News,* March 30, 2005, http://www.census.gov/Press-Release/www/releases/archives/american_community_survey_acs/004489.html (accessed March 14, 2010).

3. Los Angeles Department of Water and Power, "Neighbors Helping Neighbors Save Water," http://www.ladwp.com/ladwp/cms/ladwp012121.pdf (accessed March 14, 2010).

4. "Glen MacDonald's Water Supply," Southern California Environmental Report Card 2005, UCLA Institute of the Environment, pages 4–11, http://www.ascecareportcard.org/Outside_Source/UCLA_IOE_EnvReportCard_2005.pdf (accessed March 14, 2010).

5. Metropolitan Water District of Southern California, www.mwdh2o.com (accessed March 14, 2010).

6. Metropolitan Water District of Southern California, "Challenges and Breakthroughs," *Comprehensive Annual Financial Report*, June 30, 2008, http://www.mwdh2o.com/mwdh2o/pages/finance/CAFR%20_FY2008.pdf (accessed March 14, 2010).

7. For specifics about the mayor's greenhouse gas mitigation policies, see http://mayor.lacity.org/Issues/Environment/Climate/index.htm (accessed March 14, 2010).

8. Duke Hefland, "Officials Go with the Flow: Despite His Plea to Save Water, Mayor and Other Leaders Are Heavy Users," *Los Angeles Times*, August 10, 2007, http://articles.latimes.com/2007/aug/10/local/me-water10 (accessed March 14, 2010).

9. "Mandatory Water Conservation Is Here!" http://www.lasprinklerrepair.com/mandatory-water-conservation-is-here (accessed May 1, 2010).

10. Normal Year Water Rates, http://www.ladwp.com/ladwp/cms/ladwp001152.pdf (accessed March 14, 2010).

11. http://www.ladwp.com/ladwp/cms/ladwp001152.pdf (accessed March 14, 2010).

12. Glen Macdonald, "Hot and Dry for Decades," *Los Angeles Times*, July 13, 2007, http://www.latimes.com/news/printedition/opinion/la-oe-macdonald13jul13,1,4424613.story?coll=lanews-comment (accessed March 14, 2010).

13. Rebate Information, http://socalwatersmart.com/index.php?option=com_content&view=article&id=53&Itemid=37 (accessed March 14, 2010).

14. http://en.wikipedia.org/wiki/Reclaimed_water (accessed March 14, 2010).

15. Yoram Cohen, "Graywater—A Potential Source for Water," *Southern California Environmental Report Card*, Fall 2009, http://www.ioe.ucla.edu/report card/article.asp?parentid=4870 (accessed March 14, 2010).

16. "Achievements in Public Health, 1900–1999: Fluoridation of Drinking Water to Prevent Dental Caries," *Morbidity and Mortality Weekly Report*, October 22, 1999, http://www.cdc.gov/mmwr/preview/mmwrhtml/mm4841a1.htm (accessed March 14, 2010).

17. Sherry Glied and Matthew Neidell, "The Economic Value of Teeth," *Journal of Human Resources*, forthcoming.

18. http://en.wikipedia.org/wiki/Water_fluoridation_controversy (accessed March 14, 2010).

19. Rebecca Solnit, "California's Deficit of Common Sense," *Los Angeles Times*, November 1st 2009, http://articles.latimes.com/2009/nov/01/opinion/oe-solnit1 (accessed March 14, 2010).

20. Gary D. Libecap, *Owens Valley Revisited: A Reassessment of the West's First Great Water Transfer* (Stanford, CA: Stanford University Press, 2007).

21. http://en.wikipedia.org/wiki/Los_Angeles_County_Metro_Rail (accessed March 14, 2010).

22. http://en.wikipedia.org/wiki/New_York_City_Subway (accessed March 14, 2010).

23. http://en.wikipedia.org/wiki/London_congestion_charge (accessed March 14, 2010).

## Notes for Chapter 5

1. New York City Panel on Climate Change, "Climate Risk Information," February 2009, http://www.nyc.gov/html/planyc2030/downloads/pdf/nyc_climate_change_report.pdf (accessed March 14, 2010).

2. "Windmill Perception," September 27, 2009, http://windmillperception.posterous.com/tag/woodyallen (accessed March 14, 2010).

3. New York State Lotto Webpage, http://www.nylottery.org/ny/nyStore/cgi-bin/ProdSubEV_Cat_401_SubCat_201671_NavRoot_320.htm (accessed March 14, 2010).

4. John Lorinc, "Before the Flood," *Walrus*, June 2008, http://www.walrusmagazine.com/articles/2008.06-environment-manhattan-new-york-flood-global-warming-john-lorinc/ (accessed March 14, 2010).

5. Ibid.

6. "New York Governor Demands Answers from MTA over NYC Mass Transit Failure in Heavy Rains," *Associated Press*, August 9, 2007, http://www.foxnews.com/story/0,2933,292670,00.html (accessed March 14, 2010).

7. Sewell Chan, "Why the Subways Flood," *New York Times*, August 8, 2007, http://cityroom.blogs.nytimes.com/2007/08/08/why-do-the-subways-flood/ (accessed March 14, 2010).

8. Beth Fertig, "Ground Water: Climate Change Could Flood Subways [WYNC Interview with Cynthia Rosenzwei]," April 14, 2007, http://www.wnyc.org/news/articles/77243 (accessed March 14, 2010).

9. Statement by Mayor Michael R. Bloomberg, May 20, 2009, http://www.empire.state.ny.us/columbia/ (accessed March 14, 2010).

10. Elizabeth Dwoskin, "Columbia Ignores Peril," *Village Voice*, October 1, 2008, http://www.villagevoice.com/2008-10-01/news/everyone-listens-to-columbia-s-disaster-expert-mdash-except-columbia-itself/ (accessed March 14, 2010).

11. Ibid.

12. Ibid.

13. "Climate Risk Information."

14. "Climate Change," in *2030 New York City Plan*, http://www.nyc.gov/html/planyc2030/html/home/home.shtml (accessed March 14, 2010).

15. London Climate Change Partnership, "London's Warming," October 2002, http://www.london.gov.uk/lccp/publications/docs/londons_warming02.pdf (accessed March 14, 2010).

16. American Meteorological Society, "How Vulnerable to Flooding Is New York City?" July 31, 2008, http://www.enn.com/ecosystems/article/37813 (accessed March 14, 2010).

17. "Does the 'M' in MTA Stand for Moronic? [letter to the editor]," *New York Post*, August 12, 2007, http://www.nypost.com/p/news/opinion/letters/item_EI6oj0ydxr5MgpY2m4yXnO (accessed March 14, 2010).

18. Alexandra Lange, "Building the (New) New York," *New York Magazine*, May 28, 2006, http://nymag.com/realestate/features/2016/17143/ (accessed March 14, 2010).

19. "National Climate Change Strategy," March 2008, http://app.mewr.gov.sg/data/ImgUpd/NCCS_Full_Version.pdf (accessed March 14, 2010).

20. Lorinc, "Before the Flood."

21. Klaus Jacob, Columbia University, in Lorinc, "Before the Flood."

## Notes for Chapter 6

1. "Twenty New Cities to Be Set Up Every Year in China," *People's Daily Online*, August 14, 2000, http://english.peopledaily.com.cn/english/200008/14/eng20000814_48177.html (accessed March 14, 2010).

2. http://en.wikipedia.org/wiki/2008_Sichuan_earthquake (accessed March 14, 2010).

3. Malcolm Moore, "Chinese Earthquake May Have Been Man-made, Say Scientists," *Daily Telegraph*, February 2, 2009, http://www.telegraph.co.uk/news/worldnews/asia/china/4434400/Chinese-earthquake-may-have-been-man-made-say-scientists.html (accessed March 14, 2010).

4. "Beijing Olympic Car Ban Targets Pollution, Gridlock," *AFP*, June 19, 2008, http://afp.google.com/article/ALeqM5g9PSNBE4eCznWqSL4CdkquQHPX6A (accessed March 14, 2010).

5. "Chinese Locomotive Maker Nabs Big Deal from Turkey," *China Daily*, November 2, 2009, http://www.chinadaily.com.cn/china/2009–11/02/content_8900682.htm (accessed March 14, 2010).

6. Ibid.

7. Thomas L. Friedman, "Can I Clean Your Clock?" *New York Times*, July 4, 2009, http://www.nytimes.com/2009/07/05/opinion/05friedman.html (accessed March 14, 2010).

8. Ibid.

9. Adam Mayer, "Beijing Is China's Opportunity City," *New Geography*, August 31, 2009, http://www.newgeography.com/content/00999-beijing-chinas -opportunity-city (accessed March 14, 2010).

10. *Urbanization, Energy and Air Pollution in China: The Challenges Ahead: Proceedings of a Symposium* (Washington, DC: National Academies Press, 2004). See http://www.nap.edu/catalog.php?record_id=11192 (accessed March 14, 2010).

11. http://www.chinadaily.com.cn/bizchina/2007–11/19/content_6265825.htm (accessed March 14, 2010).

12. Siqi Zheng and Matthew E. Kahn, "Land and Residential Property Markets in a Booming Economy: New Evidence from Beijing," *Journal of Urban Economics* 63, no. 2 (2008): 743–757.

13. Siqi Zheng, Matthew E. Kahn, and Hongyu Liu, "Towards a System of Open Cities in China: Home Prices, FDI Flows and Air Quality in 35 Major Cities," *Regional Science and Urban Economics* 40, no. 1 (January 2010): 1–10.

14. Emissions Standards, http://www.implats.co.za/m/emissions.asp (accessed March 14, 2010).

15. "GM India-China Partnership," *Money*, January 1, 2010, http://www.straits times.com/BreakingNews/Money/Story/STIStory_472530.html (accessed March 14, 2010).

16. Zheng, Kahn, and Liu, "Towards a System of Open Cities in China."

17. Lau Nai-Keung, "China and the Low Carbon Economy," *China Daily*, August 20, 2009, http://www.chinadaily.com.cn/opinion/2009–08/20/content_8591605 .htm (accessed March 14, 2010).

18. "China's National Climate Change Programme" (prepared under the Auspices of National Development and Reform Commission People's Republic of China, June 2007), http://www.ccchina.gov.cn/WebSite/CCChina/UpFile/File188.pdf (accessed March 14, 2010).

19. Siqi Zheng, Rui Wang, Edward L. Glaeser, and Matthew E. Kahn, "The Greenness of China: Household Carbon Dioxide Emissions and Urban Development" (Working Paper no. 15621, National Bureau of Economic Research, 2009).

20. Grainne Ryder, "Beijing Water Supply Unaffected by 100-day Drought," *Probe International*, February 9, 2009, http://www.probeinternational.org/ beijing-water/beijings-water-supply-unaffected-100-day-drought (accessed March 14, 2010).

21. Ji Wen Hua, "Water Use and Management in Beijing" (PowerPoint presentation, December 2008), http://www.watsoninstitute.org/ge/watson_scholars/ water%20use%20and%20management%20in%20beijing.pdf (accessed March 14, 2010).

22. Chengri Deng and Gerrit Knaap, "Urban Land Policy Reform in China," *Land Lines* 15, no. 2 (April 2003), http://www.lincolninst.edu/pubs/793_Urban -Land-Policy-Reform-in-China (accessed March 14, 2010).

## Notes for Chapter 7

1. World Health Organization, "World Report on Road Traffic Injury Prevention," March 2004, http://www.who.int/violence_injury_prevention/publications/road_traffic/world_report/en/index.html (accessed March 14, 2010).

2. Yonas Abiye, "Ethiopia: Traffic Accidents, Major Public Health Crisis," *Daily Monitor*, August 3, 2009, http://allafrica.com/stories/200908031206.html (accessed March 14, 2010).

3. Raymond Guiteras, "The Impact of Climate Change on Indian Agriculture" (working paper, MIT Department of Economics, December 2007).

4. Marshall B. Burke, Edward Miguel, Shanker Satyanath, John A. Dykema, and David B. Lobell, "Warming Increases the Risk of Civil War in Africa," *PNAS* 106 (2009): 20670–20674.

5. William J. Collins and Robert A. Margo, "The Economic Aftermath of the 1960s Riots in American Cities: Evidence from Property Values," *Journal of Economic History* 67, no. 4 (2007): 849–883.

6. William Easterly, "Can Foreign Aid Buy Growth?" *Journal of Economic Perspectives* 17, no. 3 (Summer 2003): 23–48.

7. Robert Mendelsohn and Ariel Dinar, "Exploring Adaptation to Climate Change in Agriculture: The Potential of Cross-Sectional Analysis," *Agriculture and Rural Development Notes* 1 (July 2005), http://siteresources.worldbank.org/INTARD/Resources/Climate_Change_3.pdf (accessed March 14, 2010).

8. Jinxia Wang, Robert Mendelsohn, Ariel Dinar, and Jikun Huang, "How China's Farmers Adapt to Climate Change" (Working Paper 4758, World Bank Policy Research, October 2008), http://www.wds.worldbank.org/servlet/WDSContentServer/WDSP/IB/2008/10/23/000158349_20081023101522/Rendered/PDF/WPS4758.pdf (accessed March 14, 2010).

9. Joanna Kakissis, "Environmental Refugees Unable to Return Home," *New York Times*, January 5, 2010, http://greeninc.blogs.nytimes.com/2010/01/05/environmental-refugees-unable-to-return-home/ (accessed March 14, 2010).

10. Economic Research Service, U.S. Department of Agriculture, "Profiles of Tariffs in Global Agricultural Markets," http://www.ers.usda.gov/publications/aer796/aer796l.pdf (accessed March 14, 2010).

11. John Collins Rudolf, "Warming Imperils Crops in India and China," *New York Times*, January 11, 2010, http://greeninc.blogs.nytimes.com/2010/01/11/warming-imperils-crops-in-india-and-china/ (accessed March 14, 2010).

12. Dora L. Costa and Matthew E. Kahn, "Civic Engagement in Heterogeneous Communities," *Perspectives on Politics* 1, no. 1 (2003): 103–112.

13. Richard Arnott, "Housing Policy in Developing Countries: The Importance of the Informal Economy," Commission on Growth and Development (Working Paper no. 13, World Bank, 2008).

14. http://reason.com/archives/2006/02/22/hernando-de-soto-interview (accessed March 14, 2010).

15. Erica Field, "Property Rights and Investment in Urban Slums," *Journal of the European Economic Association* 3, nos. 2–3 (2005): 279–290.

16. Supriyo Nandy, "Floods in India, Disaster and Management," 2006, http://www.internationalfloodnetwork.org/AR2006/AR08Nandy.pdf (accessed March 14, 2010).

17. http://en.wikipedia.org/wiki/Cholera (accessed May 4, 2010).

18. Thomas Schelling, "What Makes Greenhouse Sense?" *Foreign Affairs* 81, no. 3 (May/June 2002): 2–9.

19. Matthew E. Kahn, "The Death Toll from Natural Disasters: The Role of Income, Geography and Institutions," *Review of Economics and Statistics* 87, no. 2 (May 2005): 271–284.

20. http://www.livescience.com/environment/disaster_deaths_1990.html (accessed March 14, 2010).

21. Derek K. Kellenberg and Ahmed Mushfiq Mobarak, 2008. "Does Rising Income Increase or Decrease Damage Risk from Natural Disasters?" *Journal of Urban Economics* 63, no. 3 (2008): 788–802.

22. "Climate Change Could Triple Population at Risk from Coastal Flooding by 2070, Finds OECD" (press release, April 12, 2007), http://www.oecd.org/document/34/0,3343,en_2649_201185_39727650_1_1_1_1,00.html (accessed March 14, 2010).

23. "Status of Kolkata Megacity Disaster Management System in View of Recent Natural Disasters," http://siteresources.worldbank.org/CMUDLP/Resources/SamanjitSengupta.pdf (accessed March 14, 2010).

24. Ibid.

25. David Satterthwaite, Saleemul Huq, Mark Pelling, Hannah Reid, and Patricia Romero Lankao, "Adapting to Climate Change in Urban Areas: The Possibilities and Constraints in Low and Medium Income Nations" (International Institute for Environment and Development, 2007), http://www.iied.org/pubs/pdfs/10549IIED.pdf (accessed March 14, 2010).

26. Timothy Besley, Robin Burgess, and Andrea Pratt, "Mass Media and Political Accountability" (working paper, LSE, 2002), http://econ.lse.ac.uk/~tbesley/papers/medbook.pdf (accessed March 14, 2010).

27. http://globalis.gvu.unu.edu/indicator_detail.cfm?IndicatorID=138&Country=VN (accessed March 14, 2010).

28. Neil Macfarquhar, "UN Reports on Developing Nations' Energy Needs," *New York Times*, September 2, 2009, http://www.nytimes.com/2009/09/02/world/02nations.html (accessed March 14, 2010).

29. Melissa Dell, Benjamin Jones, and Benjamin Olken, "Does Climate Change Affect Economic Growth?" *VOX, Research Based Policy Analysis*, http://www.voxeu.org/index.php?q=node/3633 (accessed March 14, 2010).

30. Soma Bhattacharya, Anna Alberini, and Maureen L. Cropper, "The Value of Mortality Risk Reductions in Delhi, India," *Journal of Risk and Uncertainty* 34, no. 1 (2007): 21–47; Matthew E. Kahn, "Changes in the Value of Life 1940–1980," *Journal of Risk and Uncertainty* 29, no. 2 (2004): 159–180.

31. Mark Grinblatt, Matti Keloharju, and Juhani Linnainmaa, "IQ and Stock Market Participation" (Working Paper 10-09, UCLA Anderson School, 2009).

32. James J. Heckman, "Catch 'em Young," *Wall Street Journal*, January 10, 2006, http://online.wsj.com/article/SB113686119611542381.html (accessed March 14, 2010).

33. http://offsettingbehaviour.blogspot.com/2009/11/iq-and-stock-market -participation.html (accessed March 14, 2010).

34. David Cutler and Grant Miller, "Water, Water, Everywhere: Municipal Finance and Water Supply in American Cities" (Working Paper 11096, National Bureau of Economic Research, January 2005), http://www.nber.org/papers/w11096 (accessed March 14, 2010).

35. Ibid.

36. World Wide Fund for Nature, "Mega Stress for Mega Cities: A Climate Vulnerability Ranking of Major Coastal Cities in Asia," 2007, http://assets.panda .org/downloads/mega_cities_report.pdf (accessed March 14, 2010).

## Notes for Chapter 8

1. http://www.nytimes.com/2005/10/10/science/10arctic.html?pagewanted=all (accessed March 14, 2010).

2. Adam Roberts, "Greenland, the New Bonanza," *Economist Magazine*, November 13, 2009, http://www.economist.com/displaystory.cfm?story_id= 14742475 (accessed March 14, 2010).

3. Ibid.

4. Olivier Deschenes and Enrico Moretti, "Extreme Weather Events, Mortality and Migration," *Review of Economics and Statistics* XCI, no. 4 (2009): 659–681.

5. Ellen Hanak Van Butsic and Robert G. Valletta, "Climate Change and Housing Prices: Hedonic Estimates for North American Ski Resorts" (Working Paper 2008-12, Federal Reserve Bank of San Francisco, November 2008), http://www .frbsf.org/publications/economics/papers/2008/wp08-12bk.pdf (accessed March 14, 2010).

6. Peter Fimrite, "Vast Shift in Bird Species Expected from Warming," *San Francisco Chronicle*, September 2, 2009, http://www.sfgate.com/cgi-bin/article.cgi?f =/c/a/2009/09/02/MNBT19E450.DTL (accessed March 14, 2010).

7. Richard G. Newell, Adam B. Jaffe, and Robert N. Stavins, "The Induced Innovation Hypothesis and Energy-Saving Technological Change," *The Quarterly Journal of Economics* 114, no. 3 (August 1999): 941–975.

8. http://en.wikipedia.org/wiki/Catastrophe_bond#cite_note-0 (accessed March 14, 2010).

9. Lloyds of London, "Coastal Communities and Climate Change: Maintaining Future Insurability," 2008, http://www.lloyds.com/NR/rdonlyres/33811190-E508 -4065-BB15-92EF5F3DFD41/0/360_Coastalcommunitiesandclimatechange_final.pdf (accessed March 14, 2010).

10. Gilbert Metcalf, Sergey Paltsev, John Reilly, Henry Jacoby, and Jennifer Holak, "Analysis of U.S. Greenhouse Gas Proposals" (Working Paper 13980, National Bureau of Economic Research, May 2008), http://www.nber.org/papers/ w13980 (accessed March 14, 2010).

11. A gallon of gasoline creates roughly 22 pounds of carbon dioxide. This equals (22/2000) tons; valued at $25 per ton this creates 25 X 22/2000 dollars' worth of social cost.

12. Edward L. Glaeser and Janet E. Kohlhase, "Cities, Regions and the Decline of Transport Costs" (Working Paper 9886, National Bureau of Economic Research, 2003).

13. "Berkshire Bets on U.S. with a Railroad Purchase," *New York Times*, November 3, 2009, http://dealbook.blogs.nytimes.com/2009/11/03/berkshire-to-buy -rest-of-burlington-northern-for-44-billion/?hp (accessed March 14, 2010).

14. http://en.wikipedia.org/wiki/Van_Jones (accessed March 14, 2010).

15. Elizabeth Kolbert, "Greening the Ghetto," *New Yorker*, January 12, 2009, http://www.newyorker.com/reporting/2009/01/12/090112fa_fact_kolbert (accessed March 14, 2010).

16. Ibid.

17. James J. Heckman and Jeffrey Smith, "The Sensitivity of Experimental Impact Estimates (Evidence from the National JTPA Study)," in *Youth Employment and Joblessness in Advanced Countries*, 331–356 (National Bureau of Economic Research, 2000).

18. http://www.crala.net/internet-site/Projects/Central_Industrial/CleanTech .cfm (accessed March 14, 2010).

19. Richard Beason and David E. Weinstein, "Growth, Economies of Scale, and Targeting in Japan (1955–1990)," *Review of Economics and Statistics* 78, no. 2 (1996): 286–295, http://en.wikipedia.org/wiki/Ministry_of_International_Trade_ and_Industry (accessed March 14, 2010).

20. Kevin Bullis, "A Zero-Emissions City in the Desert: Oil-rich Abu Dhabi Is Building a Green Metropolis. Should the Rest of the World Care?," *MIT Technology Review* (March/April 2009), http://www.technologyreview.com/energy/22121/?a=f (accessed March 14, 2010).

21. http://en.wikipedia.org/wiki/Dongtan (accessed March 14, 2010).

## Notes for Chapter 9

1. Camille Parmesan, "Ecological and Evolutionary Responses to Recent Climate Change," *Annual Review of Ecology, Evolution, and Systematics* 37 (December 2006): 637–669.

2. Craig Moritz, James L. Patton, Chris J. Conroy, Juan L. Parra, Gary C. White, and Steven R. Beissinger, "Impact of a Century of Climate Change on Small-Mammal Communities in Yosemite National Park, USA," *Science* 322 (October 10, 2008): 261–266.

3. "Tracking a Predator," *Washington Post*, November 3, 2009, http://www.washingtonpost.com/wp-dyn/content/graphic/2009/11/03/GR2009110303427.html (accessed March 14, 2010).

4. http://www.woodlands-junior.kent.sch.uk/Homework/adaptations/camels.htm (accessed March 14, 2010).

5. Carolyn Kousky and Roger Cooke, "Climate Change and Risk Management: Challenges for Insurance, Adaptation and Loss Estimation, Resources for the Future" (Working Paper 09-03, SSRN, 2009), http://ssrn.com/abstract=1346387 (accessed March 14, 2010).

6. Matthew E. Kahn and Michael I. Cragg, "Carbon Geography: The Political Economy of Congressional Support for Legislation Intended to Mitigate Greenhouse Gas Production" (Working Paper 14693, National Bureau of Economic Research, 2009).

7. Peter Goodman, "Emphasis on Growth Is Called Misguided," *New York Times*, September 22, 2009, http://www.nytimes.com/2009/09/23/business/economy/23gdp.html (accessed March 14, 2010).

8. Chris Bradford, blog entry, May 21, 2007, http://austinzoning.typepad.com/austincontrarian/2007/05/very_very_expen.html (accessed March 14, 2010).

# SUGGESTED FURTHER READINGS

California Electricity Commission. "Climate Change and Electricity Demand in California." By Guido Franco and Alan H. Sanstad. CEC-500-2005-201-SF. February 2006. http://www.energy.ca.gov/2005publications/CEC-500-2005-201/CEC-500-2005-201-SF.PDF (accessed March 14, 2010).

Dietz, Simon, and Nicholas Stern. "Why Economic Analysis Supports Strong Action on Climate Change: A Response to the *Stern Review*'s Critics Review of Environmental Economics and Policy." *Review of Environmental Economics and Policy* 2 (2008): 94–113.

Glaeser, Edward L. "Are Cities Dying?" *Journal of Economic Perspectives* 12, no. 2 (1998): 139–160.

Glaeser, Edward L., and Albert Saiz. "The Rise of the Skilled City." NBER Working Papers 10191. National Bureau of Economic Research, 2003.

Kahn, Matthew E. "Urban Growth and Climate Change." *Annual Review of Resource Economics* 1 (2009): 333–350.

London Climate Change Partnership. "London's Warming." October 2002. http://www.london.gov.uk/lccp/publications/docs/londons_warming02.pdf (accessed March 14, 2010).

"London's Response to Climate Change." http://www.london.gov.uk/shaping-london/london-plan/docs/chapter5.pdf (accessed March 14, 2010).

Metcalf, Gilbert E. "Designing a Carbon Tax to Reduce U.S. Greenhouse Gas Emissions." *Review of Environmental Economics and Policy* 3 (2009): 63–83.

New York City Panel on Climate Change. "Climate Risk Information." February 2009. http://www.nyc.gov/html/planyc2030/downloads/pdf/nyc_climate_change_report.pdf (accessed March 14, 2010).

Satterthwaite, David, Saleemul Huq, Mark Pelling, Hannah Reid, and Patricia Romero Lankao. "Adapting to Climate Change in Urban Areas: The Possibilities and Constraints in Low and Medium Income Nations." July 2007. http://www.iied.org/pubs/pdfs/10549IIED.pdf (accessed March 14, 2010).

Weitzman, Martin. "Some Basic Economics of Extreme Climate Change." 2009. http://www.economics.harvard.edu/faculty/weitzman/files/Cournot%2528Weitzman%2529.pdf (accessed March 14, 2010).

Zheng, Siqi, Rui Wang, Edward L. Glaeser, and Matthew E. Kahn. "The Greenness of China: Household Carbon Dioxide Emissions and Urban Development." NBER Working Papers 15621. National Bureau of Economic Research, Inc., 2009.

# INDEX

AB32 (California), 210
Abu Dhabi, 222–223
Adaptation, 6–7, 230, 233, 235
  in China, 151, 153, 158
  at Columbia University, 119
  in developing countries, 185, 187
  and economic development,
    179–183
  in environmentalist cities, 68,
    107
  farmers and, 99, 161
  government policies, 74, 81, 93,
    110, 151
  and innovation, 8, 198–202, 228
  and insurance industry, 206
  and international trade, 195
  in LDCs, 178
  market for, 236
  in New York City, 121
  of other species, 227
  paying for, 134–137
  and the poor, 128
  to population increases, 9
  and prices, 90, 110
  products, 13, 200, 236
  public support for, 41
  to sea level rise, 61
  strategy, 166
Affleck, Ben, 113
Agnew, John, 30
Agriculture, 166
Air conditioners, 60, 112, 198, 202,
  235

Air pollution, 74, 84, 85, 141, 145,
  150, 228
Allen, Woody, 113
Alper, Andrew, 129
Alpine flora, 226
Amazon.com, 196
American Clean Energy and
  Security Act, 209
Appliances, energy-efficient, 94,
  216
Arbitrage, 196, 197
Arizona, 192, 194
*Armageddon* (motion picture), 113
Arnott, Richard, 167

Baltimore, 213
Baumann, Frederick, 37
Becker, Gary, 11
Behavioral economists, 10–11
Beijing, 75, 140, 141, 144, 146, 147,
  153–154, 177
*Bell Curve, The* (Murray), 183
Berkeley (California), 67–68, 69,
  149
Berkeley, University of California,
  220
Berlin, 75
Beverly Hills, 107
Big business, 93
Birds, 226, 227
Birth rate, 176, 177
Black market activity, 27
Bloomberg, Michael, 121–122

Boston, 47–48, 57, 67, 69–70, 106, 115, 137, 190, 213, 220
*Brave New World* (Huxley), 183
Bronx (New York City), 129, 190–191
Brooklyn (New York City), 129
Bubble Yum (bubble gum), 66
Buffalo, 53, 73, 190, 194, 213
Buffett, Warren, 213
Building codes, 33 34, 37, 68, 121. *See also* Zoning
Burlington Northern Santa Fe railroads, 213
Bush, George W., 36
Butterflies, 226

Calcutta, 172, 173, 186
Calcutta Municipal Coporation, 173
Calgary, 75
California, 61, 80, 82, 83
    carbon emissions, 210, 211
    and carbon mitigation regulation, 237
    farmers as water source, 97–99
    fire risk due to climate change, 99–102
    "green tech" industries, 219
    greenhouse gas emissions, 210, 211, 214
    heat wave (2006), 192
    sea level rise, 60
    ski industry, 194
    transportation sector, 214
    water shortage, 89, 90–95, 97, 99
    *See also individual cities*
Calvin, William, 15
Camels, 227
Canadian Rocky Mountains, 226
Canals, 173
Cap and trade, 210
Capital, LDCs' access to, 185–186
Capitalism, 26

and adaptation to climate change, 7
as cause of climate change, 3, 149, 201
and cities, 2
cynicism about, 65
development of new products, 199
evolutionary nature of, 234–236
and government intervention, 209
Carbon dioxide, 3, 71, 211, 222
Carbon footprints, 105
Carbon mitigation, 5, 70, 201
    in China, 143, 148, 153
    in LDCs, 178
    products, 200
    regulation, 214, 230, 236–237, 238
Carbon pricing, 176, 212, 213, 214, 219
Carbon taxes, 72, 104, 201, 210, 212, 213, 219, 236, 237
Carter, Jimmy, 229
Catastrophe bonds, 204–205
CCSM Model, 82
Central London Congestion Charge, 106
Cheney, Dick, 69
Chicago, 80, 213
    cold-related deaths in, 193
    heat wave (1995), 84
    shift from manufacturing to services, 55
Chicago Fire (1871), 17–18, 37
Chile, 170
China, 139–158
    adaptation to climate change, 155
    air pollution in, 145
    Communist Party, 155
    difference from United States, 137

ecocity, 223
and economic development, 187, 212
electric power in, 149–151
and international trade, 195
per capita carbon emissions, 140, 153
public transportation, 144
China Lithium Energy Investment Group, 142
*Chinatown* (motion picture), 98
Cholera, 169, 184
Churchill, Winston, 12
Cincinnati, 213
Cities
competition between, 48
diversity between, 7–8
diversity within, 40, 128, 166–167
most climate resilient, 73–75
recovery after disasters, 17–21
with small carbon footprints, 71–72
*Civil Action, A* (motion picture), 63
Civil war, 162
Clean Air Act, 85, 86–87, 146–147
Clean Energy Corps Working Group, 217
Cleveland, 48, 53, 190, 191, 193, 194, 213
Climate amenity, 83–84
Climate bundle, 83
Climate models, 56–57, 232, 241
for Africa, 162
and insurance industry, 205, 206, 207–208
for Los Angeles, 82, 83, 100, 233
for New York City, 113, 115, 123
for Phoenix, 193, 234
for Pittsburgh, 193
Clinton, Hillary, 21
Coal, 210–211

Coastal cities, 57–58, 62, 63, 136, 137, 152, 158, 172, 185, 228, 242
Coda Automotive, 53
Coffee analogy, 89
Cold waves, 192
Colorado, 194
Columbia University, 38, 117, 118–120, 125
Common threats, 39
Communist Party, 152, 155
Community Climate System Model (CCSM), 57
Copenhagen Climate Conference, 209
Coping strategies, 100
Corruption, 175
Creative destruction, 17
Creativity, 38
CSR Zhuzhou Electric Locomotive Co. (China), 142
Cuban immigration, 42–43, 232
Culture of waste, 88

Dallas, 53
Damascus, Syria, 16
Davis, Donald, 19–20
de Soto, Hernando, 168
Dell, Melissa, 180–181
Demand-side conservation, 93
Demand, 135, 235
for electricity, 59, 60, 109–110, 112, 201, 223
for fuel-efficient vehicles, 212
for gasoline, 212
for housing, 35, 43, 105, 135, 231
and insurance industry, 134, 204
for new products, 8, 35, 69, 120, 178, 234, 235, 236
transportation, 106, 109
for water, 93, 154, 234
*See also* Supply and demand

Democracy Corps, 40

Denmark, 58

Density, population, 104–105, 106–108, 108–109, 112, 128, 168, 171, 177, 187

Deschenes, Olivier, 192

Despommier, Dickson D., 240

Detroit, 48, 53, 56, 73, 190, 191, 193, 213, 216, 240

Developing world, 159–187, 230

Dhaka, 186

Diamond, Jared, 2–3

Diesel fuel, 212

Disasters
as economic opportunities, 24
recovery from, 15–16
*See also* Natural disasters

Disease, infectious, 169

Distraction of U.S. public, 23

Dongfeng Motor Corp. (China), 142

Dongtan (China), 223

Driver, Minnie, 99

Drought, 234, 239, 242

Ducat, Arthur, 37

Earth Institute (Columbia University), 118

Earthquakes, 109, 140–141, 170–171

Economic development
and adaptation, 179–183
and death count from natural disasters, 171
in developing countries, 187
and education, 170
and greenhouse gas emissions, 176
and public health, 170

Economic growth
and education, 182
effect of temperatures on, 180–181
and pollution production, 149

Education, 68, 146, 170, 174, 182

Ehrlich, Paul, 9

Eisensee, Thomas, 23

Electric vehicles, 142

Electricity, 71, 72, 178, 198, 222
in China, 150, 151, 153, 157
consumption, 95, 104, 201
demands, 59, 60, 109–110, 112, 201, 223
in developing countries, 178
in Houston, 71–72
prices, 68, 81, 90, 110, 167, 201–202, 211, 215, 219, 230

Emissions standards, 147, 214

Energy demand, 60

Energy efficiency, 219

Energy technology, 142

Engineering, 96–97, 109, 130–134, 147–148, 154, 214. *See also* Technology

England, 48, 74

Environmental refugees, 164

Environmentalism, 146

*Erin Brockovich* (motion picture), 65

Esperanza's Community Health Programs, 85

European Union (EU), 58

Evolution, 15–16, 226

Exports, 152

Fairness, sense of, 205–206

False sense of security, 131–132

Fargo (North Dakota), 51–52, 56, 136

Farmers
how they cope with climate conditions, 161, 162–164
as water source, 97–99

Farms, vertical, 240

Favoritism, 152–153

Federal Emergency Management Agency (FEMA), 117, 119

Fertility patterns, 176–177
Field, Erica, 168
Financial innovation, 204–205
Financial risk taking, 38
Finland, 182
Finnish Central Securities
      Depository Registry, 182
Fireman's Insurance Company,
      37–38
Fires, 99–102, 228
Flea (Red Hot Chili Peppers), 99–100
Floating houses, 34–35, 61, 231
Flood plains, building in, 27–33
Flooding, 61, 115–116, 119, 131,
      132, 171, 173, 206, 239
Florida
   adaptation in, 197
   building codes in, 33, 34
   improvement in climate bundle,
      83
   and insurance industry, 33,
      204–205
   real estate values, 33, 34
   water rights, 154
Fluoride, 96–97
Food chain, 239–240
Food production shocks, 174–175
Forecasts, 232, 233
Foreign aid, 162
Foreign direct investment (FDI), 148
Fort Lauderdale, 83
France, 192
Free market, 25, 45
Free riders, 4
Freight trains, 212
Friedman, Milton, 11, 31
Friedman, Tom, 142–143
Fuel economy standards, 147, 214

Gambling analogy, 31
Gasoline, 212
Gasoline tax, 104, 236

Gates, Bill, 41
General Motors, 148
Geography, 179–180
Germany, 20, 48, 180
Gillespie, Tom, 30
Giuliani, Rudy, 36, 54, 235
Global Report on Human Settlements
      (United Nations), 164
Golf courses, private, 108–109
Google, 200, 231, 235, 236, 239
   Google China, 139, 220
   Google Earth, 30
   and Stanford, 182
Gore, Al, 9, 11–12, 67, 68, 69, 70, 71
Government, 174–175, 208–209
   (state providing useful public
      goods), 187
   local, 173
   mandates, 208
   policies, 45, 81, 93, 110
   regulation, 134, 206
Government intervention, 23–27, 45
   as cause of more risk, 27–33
Gray water, reuse of, 96
Great Depression, 25
Great Lakes, 57–58
Green for All, 217
Greenhouse gas emissions, 140,
      141–142, 150, 176, 178, 209,
      210, 214, 219, 229
   carbon emissions, 3–4, 69, 70,
      71, 210, 211–212, 219, 230, 237
   and economic development, 176
Greenland, 191–192
Greenspan, Alan, 231
Grinnell, Joseph, 226
Growth controls, 106–108
Guns, Germs, and Steel (Diamond), 2

H3A1FI Model, 82
Haiti, 170
Health, and wealth, 170

Heat waves, 180, 192, 228, 239
Heckman, James, 183
Homeowners, 44
Hong Kong, 137, 157, 158
Hong Kong Administrative Region
    Basic Law Committee, 150
Houston, 69, 70, 71–72, 81, 112
Hukou (Chinese registration
    system), 144
Human capital, 170, 177
Hurricane Frances (2004), 116
Hurricane Katrina (New Orleans),
    16, 22, 34, 36, 39, 40, 45
Hurricanes, 118, 228
Huxley, Aldous, 183
Hybrid vehicles, 142

Ice caps, melting, 191–192
Immigrants, 128–129, 216
Immigration, 232
Incentives, 11, 94, 101, 102, 104,
    105, 106, 157, 199, 213
Income, per capita, 3, 24, 140, 153,
    155, 180, 230, 239
India, 174–175, 212
Indiana, 211
Individualism, 41
Information, real-time, 201
Infrastructure, 33, 105, 116–117,
    121, 128, 135, 137, 143, 144,
    167–168, 173, 175, 177, 184,
    185, 242
Innovation, 8, 96, 198–202,
    204–205, 214, 235
Inside information, 65, 66
Institutions, 179–180, 180
Insurance, 37, 100–101, 133–134,
    202–209, 228, 235
Intellectual property, 178
International trade, 148–149, 165,
    172, 195–196
Internet, 53

Invention, necessity as mother of,
    200
Investments, 161, 172, 181, 184,
    185, 186, 187, 190
Iowa, 57

Jacksonville (Florida), 82
Jacob, Klaus, 118–119, 120
Jakarta, 186
Japan, 19–20, 187, 221
Jelly bean analogy, 221
Jersey City, 213
Jeter, Derek, 110
Jilin, 153
Job training, 218
Jobs Training Partnership Act
    (JTPA), 218
Jones, Benjamin, 180–181
Jones, Van, 217, 218

Keynes, John Maynard, 25, 26, 218
Knight, Frank, 48
Koi ponds, 87
Kolbert, Elizabeth, 11, 217
Krakow, 75
Krugman, Paul, 6

Lagos, 173
Lake Tahoe, 194
Land assembly, 28–29
Land, price of, 155–156
Land use regulators, 133
Land values, 126, 155–156
Landowners, 194
Las Vegas, 51, 53, 83
Lau Nai-keung, 150
Leadership, 36
Legislation, carbon-pricing, 213
Less developed countries (LDCs),
    168–169, 176, 178, 179, 183,
    185–186
Levison, J. B., 37

Life expectancy, 184
Life Savers (candy maker), 66
Limbaugh, Rush, 67, 242
Literacy, 175. *See also* Education
London, 55–56, 106, 115, 122, 131, 137, 207, 232
Long Beach (California), 91
Los Angeles, 74, 77–93
   climate forecasts, 82, 83, 100, 232, 233
   fire risk, 100
   population density, 104–105
   public transit, 102–105
   real estate in, 190, 233
   Red Line subway, 103
   traffic congestion, 105
   water pricing, 92–93, 110
   water shortage, 91–92, 96
Los Angeles Country Club, 108
Louisville, 213

MacArthur, Douglas, 235
Make It Right Foundation, 34
Malaria, 169, 180, 181
Malaysia, 169–170
Malibu, 107
Mammals, 226, 227
Manchester (England), 48, 55
Manhattan, 104–105, 108, 111–137, 240, 241. *See also* New York City
Manhattanville Project (Columbia University), 117
Manila, 186
Manufacturing, 21, 53, 55–56, 148, 215
Maps, 30
Mariel boatlift (1980), 42, 44, 232
Marina Barrage, 131
Markets
   free, 25, 45
   global, 196, 199

Marshall Plan, 16, 22
Masdar (Abu Dhabi), 222–223
Masdar Initiative, 222
Massachusetts Institute of Technology, 161
Mayne, Thom, 34, 35, 230–231
McConaughey, Matthew, 99
Media, 22–23, 68, 174, 214
Medicare, 41
Melting ice caps, 191–192
Metropolitan Water District of Southern California, 89
Miami, 42–43, 44
Mianyang, 153
Migration, 12, 43, 52, 53, 58
   coastal, 58
   away from coastal areas, 61
   to China, 144–145, 156
   of jobs, 124, 125
   to Manhattan, 114, 129
   of manufacturing, 21
   away from New Orleans, 22
   patterns, 233
   in response to shocks, 41–45
   rural-to-urban, 144, 156, 160–161, 162, 164, 216
   of senior citizens, 57, 74
   to the Sun Belt, 193
   *See also* Voting with feet
Milan (Italy), 49
Milwaukee, 73, 213
Ministry of International Trade and Industry (MITI, Japan), 221
Minneapolis, 73, 193, 213
Mississippi, 216
Missouri, 211, 237
Mitigation
   agenda, 5, 148
   carbon, 70, 71, 143, 148, 153, 214, 230, 237
   in China, 143, 148, 153
   climate change, 70, 143, 190, 201

Mitigation *(continued)*
  in LDCs, 178
  policies, 236, 238
  products, 200
  regulation, 70, 214, 237
  of risk, 135, 184
Montana, 194
Moretti, Enrico, 192
Moscow, 75
Move to Opportunity (MTO)
  program, 62–63
Mudanjiangg, 153
Mumbai, 149, 172
Murmansk (Russia), 191
Murray, Charles, 183

Natural disasters
  and adaptation, 230
  deaths from, 170–171
  in developing world, 158, 160,
    170–173, 186
  influence of mass media on
    government response to, 23
  and innovation, 34
  precautionary investments, 136
  predictions of, 242
  and regulatory codes, 34
  urban damage caused by, 172–173
  *See also* Disasters
Necessity, mother of invention, 143,
  200
Neoclassical economists, 11
Netherlands, 58
Nevada, 194
New Mexico, 194
New Orleans, 213
  and floating homes, 34
  future of, 40
  government assistance, 16, 22,
    23, 25, 27, 33
  migration away from, 22
  ninth ward, 62

New York City, 47–48, 50, 74, 135,
  158, 213, 221, 241
  carbon footprint, 105, 112
  crime rate, 54–55
  after 9/11, 16, 38, 39
  public transit, 106
  real estate values, 190
  shift from manufacturing to
    services, 55
  *See also* Manhattan
New York City Climate Change
  Adaptation Task Force, 121
New York City Panel on Climate
  Change (NPCC), 121
New York State, economic hardship
  in, upstate, 21–22
New York University, 38, 125
Newark, 213
Newsom, Gavin, 67
NGOs (non-governmental
  organizations), 84–85, 164
Nicholson, Jack, 98
NIMBYism (not in my back yard),
  72
North Dakota, 51, 57
North Korea, 180

Obama, Barack, 209, 217
Ohio, 211
Olken, Benjamin, 180–181
Olympic Games, 23, 141
Organization for Economic
  Cooperation and
  Development, 172
Ozone, 85, 86

Pacific Institute, 60, 61–62
Pacific Palisades, 107
Palmer, Potter, 37
Paris, 75
Per capita income, 3, 24, 140, 153,
  155, 180, 230, 239

Philadelphia, 213
Phoenix, 53, 74, 193, 234
Pitt, Brad, 34, 35
Pittsburgh, 55, 193, 213
PlaNYC 2030 project, 121
Policies, 97, 100, 102, 104, 110, 152,
    167, 168, 219, 236
Politics, 68
Pollution, 149, 239
Pollution permits, 210
Pollution tax, 211
Poor immigrants, 84, 86–87
Poor minorities, 86–87
Population
    age of, 74
    U.S., 53
    world, 3, 230
*Population Bomb* (Ehrlich), 9
Population density, 104–105,
    106–108, 108–109, 112, 128,
    168, 171, 177, 187
Population growth, 176–177
Portland, 67
Poverty rate, 195
Power grids, 112
Price gouging, 206, 207, 208
Price signals, 209
Prices, 89–90, 90–93, 95, 96,
    109–110, 135, 196, 199, 201,
    202, 209
    carbon, 219
    electricity, 68, 81, 90, 110, 167,
        201–202, 211, 215, 219, 230
    gasoline, 212
    for goods and services, 235
    insurance, 134
    land, 126, 155–156
    real estate, 233
    rising, 235
    water, 81, 90–93, 96, 110, 234,
        236
Pricing schedules, 94

Prison inmates, 101–102
Private-sector investment, 23–24
Property rights, 168
Protests, 156
Providence, 213
Public health
    Chicago heat wave (1995), 84
    in China, 150
    in coastal cities, 49
    and decline in pollution, 147
    in developing countries,
        168–170
    improvements in, 147
    intervention, 97
    and public service
        announcements, 84
    and urban population growth,
        168–170, 184
Public investments, 185. *See also*
    Government
Public sector, 218
Public transit, 72, 102–106, 112,
    115–116, 126–128, 235
Public Utilities Board (PUB), 130
Public-works programs, 217

Quality of life, 54–56, 126, 157,
    183, 190, 195, 216, 219, 220,
    229, 238, 242
Queens (New York City), 112, 125,
    129

Railroads, 213
Rainfall, 57, 83
Rational expectations, 11, 156
Rationing, 91
Reading (England), 48
Reagan, Ronald, 73, 229
Real estate, 82, 108, 190, 233
Rebates, 94
Redistribution, 39–40, 41
Refugees, environmental, 164

Regulation, 85, 86–87, 108, 133, 134, 147, 149, 210, 214, 215, 230, 237
Research universities, 220
Risk, 129, 159–160, 181, 187, 241
  adapting to, 61, 153
  and Columbia University, 119
  cover-ups, 64, 66
  in developing world, 159–160, 171, 185
  of flooding, 132–133, 171
  and government protection, 31
  and land prices, 155–156
  in New Orleans, 40
  in New York City, 113–115, 132–133
  unquantified, 113–115, 229
  and urban poor, 40
  vehicle emissions, 85
Risk allocation markets, 202–205
Risk mitigation, 135, 184
Riviera Country Club, 108
Roberts, Adam, 192
Roberts, Julia, 65
Rural areas, 239–240
Rust Belt, 193, 237

Sachs, Jeff, 120, 180
Salt Lake City, 73, 74
San Diego, 56, 57, 59–60, 83, 135, 158
San Francisco, 67, 71, 72, 74, 83, 135, 167, 213
San Francisco earthquake (1906), 37
Santa Ana winds, 99, 100
Santa Monica (California), 53, 107, 167
Santa Monica Big Blue bus, 102
Schelling, Thomas, 123, 169
Schumpeter, Joseph, 17
Schwarzenegger, Arnold, 214, 215

Sea level, 73, 172, 241
  adaptation to sea level rise, 58
  of California coast, 60–61
  and carbon mitigation, 237
  and Columbia University, 120
  and engineering measures, 130
  and insurance industry, 206, 228
  and melting ice, 191
  of New York City, 115, 120, 241
  of San Diego, 59
  of Singapore, 130, 158
Sea walls, 32–33, 135, 187
Seattle, 67
Seinfeld, 218
Sen, Amartya, 239
Service employment, 55–56
Shanghai, 137, 140, 152, 153, 156, 157–158
Shanghai Automotive Industry Corp., 148
Sharks, 226
Shocks, 174–175, 197, 198, 239, 241
Siberia, 226
Sichuan earthquake, 140–141
Sierra Club, 71
Sierra Mountains, 89
Silicon Valley, 220
Simpson, Homer, 10, 11–12, 110, 183, 227, 236
Singapore, 115, 130, 169–170
Ski industry, 194
Smart grid, 201
Smith, Adam, 230, 235
Smog, 81, 84, 85–87, 104, 107
Social Security, 41
Solar power, 67, 68, 69, 107, 150, 211, 216, 222, 240
South Korea, 180, 187
Soviet Union, 154
Spain, 226
Spelling, Candy, 92, 93, 110

Sprawl, 72, 79
Sri Lanka, 163
St. Louis (Missouri), 27–28, 29, 31, 33, 54, 101, 213
Standard of living, 10, 129, 183, 184, 223, 238
Standards, emissions, 147, 214
Stanford, 220
Stiglitz, Joe, 120, 239
Streisand, Barbra, 107
Strömberg, David, 23
Subsidies, 29, 94, 104, 110, 136, 142, 217, 221. *See also* Government intervention
Sumatra, 15
Sun Belt, 193
Supply and demand, 42, 89, 90–91, 109–110, 134, 135, 234
Suqian, 153
Swimming pools, 90

Tariffs, 165
Taxes, 26, 27, 102, 104, 124, 135, 208, 210, 211, 219, 236, 237. *See also* Carbon taxes
Technology, 69, 130–134, 177, 178
    advances, 60, 125
    breakthroughs, 147–148
    clean, 5
    energy, 142
    fixes, 152
    geo-engineering, 5, 10
    innovation, 214
    water, 96
    *See also* Engineering
Telephone communication, 178
Temperature, 237, 241
    average, 10, 51, 57, 241
    in California, 83, 101
    and carbon levels, 10
    and civil war, 162
    and ecosystems, 225–226
    effect on economic growth, 180–181
    effect on flora, 226
    and farming, 161, 163, 164, 181
    and fire risk, 101
    in Florida, 83
    global, 10, 15
    in Los Angeles, 82, 83
    and malaria, 169
    and mortality, 192, 193
    in New York City, 112–113, 122
    in poor countries, 180–181
    and poor immigrants, 84
    in San Diego, 59
    summer, 193
    winter, 193
Terrorist attacks (9/11/2001), 36, 38, 39
Thames River, 122, 131
"Theft of Owens Valley," 98
Thornton, Billy Bob, 113
Thyphoid, 184
*Titanic* analogy, 4–5
Tongliao, 153
Torre, Joe, 110
Tourism, 55, 56, 66
Trade, international, 148–149, 165, 172, 195–196
Transportation sector, 214
Travolta, John, 64
Treelines, 226
Trucking industry, 211–212
Trump, Donald, 126, 181
Trump, Donald Jr., 132
Tsinghua University, 139–140, 220
Tulane University, 40
Twitter, 54
Typhoid, 184

Unemployment, 26, 216, 217
United Kingdom, 58
United Nations, 178

Urban growth, 153
Urban minorities, 62, 217
Urban poor, 40, 62, 128–129, 156, 160, 164–168, 219, 242–243
Urbanization, 168–170, 176–177, 230
U.S. Army Corps of Engineers, 123
U.S. Environmental Protection Agency (EPA), 146
U.S. Housing and Urban Development, 62

Vehicle emissions, 85, 86
Vehicles, 142, 144, 212, 216
Venezuela, 167
Venice (California), 65–66, 107, 130
Venice (Italy), 49
Vietnam, birth rate, 176
Vietnam War, impact on growth of cities, 20–21
Villaragosa, Tony, 90
Violence, 161–162
Volcanoes, 15
Voting with feet, 42, 43, 48, 52, 157, 234. See also Migration

Wall Street, 124, 125, 126, 129, 186, 220
Washington, D.C., 81, 106, 135, 213
Waste, culture of, 88
Water, 88–99
    desalinization, 96, 152, 228, 235
    diversion of, 154
    farmers as source of, 97–99

polluted urban, 169
price of, 81, 90–93, 96, 110, 234, 236
shortage of, 97
supply, 96
transfers, 98
wastage, 88
Wealth, 146, 170
Weinstein, David, 19–20
West Los Angeles, 108–109. See also Los Angeles
West Palm Beach, 83
Willis, Bruce, 113
Wind farms, 150
Wind power, 211
Wind turbines, 240
Winner's curse, 221
Winter, 75, 81, 82, 193, 194, 219
Women, employment opportunities of, 177
World Bank, 162, 163
World Health Organization, 159
World War II, 16, 22
Wyoming, 194

Yosemite National Park, 226

Zero-impact cities, 222–223
Zipingpu Dam, 140–141
Zoning, 62, 73, 102, 108, 133–134, 209, 242. See also Building codes